THE **21st** Century Sunday School

THE 21st Century Sunday School

Strategies for Today and Tomorrow

WES HAYSTEAD

STANDARD
PUBLISHING
Cincinnati, Ohio

The Standard Publishing Company, Cincinnati, Ohio
A division of Standex International Corporation
© 1995 by Wesley Haystead
All rights reserved
Printed in the United States of America

02 01 00 99 98 97 96 95   5 4 3 2 1

All charts, worksheets, diagrams, and job descriptions indicated by the ✎ symbol in the table of contents **are intended to be reproduced for ministry purposes** only—not for resale.

Editorial team: Mark A. Taylor, Kristi Walter, Linda Ford, Shirley Beegle
Cover design by SchultzWard
Page design by Robert E. Korth

Library of Congress Cataloging-in-Publication Data

Haystead, Wesley.

    The 21st century Sunday School : strategies for today and tomorrow
/   by Wes Haystead
         p.   cm.
    ISBN 0-7847-0394-9
    1. Sunday schools.   I. Title
BV1521.H38   1995   95-1317
268—dc20   CIP

This book is dedicated to Lowell Brown, whose lifelong commitment to the teaching ministry of the church has made a powerful impact on thousands of teachers and leaders.

21st
Century
Sunday
School

Contents

✎ denotes a reproducible
chart, worksheet, diagram,
or job description.

✐ denotes a reproducible
chart, worksheet, diagram,
or job description.

✎ denotes a reproducible chart, worksheet, diagram, or job description.

Introduction

The church is moving into the twenty-first century.

Looking ahead, to see how the 2000s will be different from the 1900s is a risky, yet fascinating challenge. Since no one really knows for sure what life will be like in the third millennium, nor how long God will allow human history to extend, this book is not an attempt to peer into the future and make predictions. This book is, however, a call for local congregations to consider one very important question: How will we communicate the essential elements of the Christian faith in ways that speak to life in this new millennium?

For more than two centuries, churches of all denominations, sizes, and styles have relied heavily, with admittedly mixed results, on the Sunday school as its agency for such communication. During the latter part of the twentieth century, many church leaders sought other means of teaching people, often neglecting and in some cases abandoning the Sunday school. However, no other agency of the church has been successful in replacing the Sunday school as a widely accepted and effective means of education, fellowship, and outreach.

Many church leaders are giving a renewed emphasis to Sunday school, declaring that the venerable institution has value and potential. However, even the Sunday school's strongest supporters have questioned whether the traditional Sunday school structures are still the best way for the church to pursue its mission of reaching and discipling people in our ever-changing society.

Since you are reading this book, it seems safe to assume that you share a concern for the teaching ministries of the church. It is only fair to let you know that this book contains no startling predictions of what life in the third millennium will be like. Nor does it say anything about the time or sequence of events surrounding the second coming.

The purpose of this manual is threefold.

First, it will raise some issues that churches must explore in evaluating and planning their present and future teaching ministries.

Second, it will provide some perspectives to aid in considering the potential results of various approaches to those issues.

Third, it will suggest approaches for building and leading a Sunday school that will continue to be effective in the coming century.

The Sunday School and Other Teaching Ministries

Because the Sunday school is the largest and most familiar local church ministry for reaching and teaching, it is the focus of this manual. At the same time, most of the numerous other discipleship ministries, whether conducted on the church premises or in homes or other locations, whether meeting on Sunday or at other times of the week, whether involving multiple age groups or just children or youth or adults, all share most of the same challenges and opportunities as the Sunday school. All ministries that seek to reach people and then to teach them face similar issues in planning how to meet the changing needs of congregations, communities, and individuals. Thus, this manual, while using the familiar terminology of the Sunday school, will address the whole scope of

the local church's mission to "go and make disciples" (Matthew 28:19).

The Sunday School and Other Volunteer Agencies

The Sunday school is significantly impacted by the forces at work in contemporary society. This is partly because the Sunday school is an organization, similar to many others in our society, and partly because it deals every week with issues of daily living. The last three decades of the twentieth century saw a big decline in the number of volunteers who worked in community agencies such as the Red Cross and Boy Scouts. Should anyone be surprised to find that during those same years, church leaders found it increasingly difficult to enlist people in teaching ministries?

Robert Putnam of Harvard University contends that the closing decades of the twentieth century have been marked by a measurable decrease in social interaction and commitment. While there are notable exceptions, Putnam cites numerous indicators that people are less likely today than in earlier generations to join with others in pursuing the common good.* To the extent the people of the church are influenced by factors shaping society, the church's programs are subject to the same challenges as other groups.

Our society and our church have never been in greater need of the ministry of the Sunday school. Sadly, the church has rarely been less able and willing to provide the quality of ministry that is needed. This manual is written to aid the local church in providing teaching and discipling ministries that effectively meet the needs of people today and in the future.

* Robert Putnam, "Bowling Alone," *The Journal of Democracy*, January 1995.

1
Where Is Your Sunday School Going?

The chart was great! It was big, big enough to cover a multitude of pinholes, plaster cracks, and paint chips on the wall of our Sunday school office. It was professionally designed and printed, which made a nice contrast to all the hand-lettered signs posted in the room. It was attractive with appealing pictures of wholesome-looking children, young people, and adults. It was impressive, clearly outlining the biblical knowledge and spiritual truths that the students in our Sunday school would gain over a lifetime of involvement.

Not only was the chart great, it was free! Our nice publishing company had sent it to us to help us clearly see where the weeks and months and years of Sunday school instruction was taking us. There was an adorable, chubby little two-year-old and a list of the Bible characters he would meet. A cute, blonde three-year-old beamed at

us over the column of content she would master. This continued, column after column, age after age, right up to some very earnest-looking adults whose demeanor exuded the wealth of good teaching they received through the Sunday school.

It was 1963 and the Sunday school was still basking in its "Golden Age" of growth and expansion that had marked the forties and fifties. As a young, enthusiastic officer of an active, growing Sunday school, I sat and meditated on that chart, proud to be part of a ministry with such a rich heritage, one that knew what its mission was and how it was going to accomplish it.

Then our pastor walked into the room and followed my gaze toward the chart. Certain that he would be impressed with such obvious evidence of my organized approach to leadership, I waited for a suitable word of commendation.

Leaning in toward the chart, he poked a finger at one of the columns. "What happens if I miss a few Sundays in here?" Jabbing at another column, he said, "What if I first start coming around here?" Following his drawing of an invisible circle around one whole column, he asked, "Suppose I just don't like the teacher I'm assigned while I'm supposed to be learning this?" He stepped back and took in the whole scope of the chart. "Where do we get the teachers who are really capable of achieving all this?"

His gaze shifted from the chart to me. I hoped he didn't notice the beads of sweat that were decorating my forehead. I also hoped that he didn't notice my relief when he smiled, patted my shoulder, and said, "Nice chart," as he walked out of the office.

Suddenly, charting the course of a Sunday school was not as clearly defined a task as I had thought. Today, after thirty years of involvement with the Sunday school, after leading five Sunday schools in five different churches, after conducting hundreds of training sessions for thousands of teachers and leaders, and after writing books, articles, and curriculum resources for use in Sunday schools, I believe the challenges of Sunday school leadership are more diverse than ever.

Leading a Sunday school in positive, effective ministry has always been more complex than any chart could illustrate. Any program that involves a wide range of age levels, that is operated and led mostly, if not entirely, by volunteers, that meets every week all year around, and that looks to the Bible as its major textbook, could never be a simple endeavor. Even though other reaching and discipling agencies (Vacation Bible School, club programs, home Bible studies, youth groups, etc.) can more narrowly focus their efforts, they all share a similar challenge: to make a continuing positive impact and to avoid simply operating religious machinery.

Where should we be leading our church's teaching ministries in the years ahead? What should we define as goals to pursue, teaching strategies to implement, and organizational structures to establish? Which aspects of our church's current efforts need to be continued; which should be modified or discarded in light of the changes that surround us? How can we nurture and communicate a vision that will serve us well in the uncertainties of the future?

Before we explore where the Sunday school and other similar ministries should be going, it will be helpful to gain some perspective by looking back.

A Brief Review of Sunday School History

Church history contains numerous records of organized teaching efforts. These efforts have been linked to outreach efforts in new areas, and they have emphasized nurturing the spiritual life of the church. While the Sunday school can trace its heritage back over many centuries through a host of teaching ministries, the credit for launching the modern Sunday school movement belongs to a wealthy English newspaper publisher, Robert Raikes.

Raikes began his first Sunday school in 1780 in the kitchen of a private home in the slums of Gloucester. The first students were very poor, uneducated children who spent six days a week working in deplorable factory conditions. Raikes' school began in the morning, broke for lunch, then continued through the afternoon. A healthy dose of biblical instruction was given along with instruction in reading and writing. The goal was to change the inner character of these children and as a result, to make a positive impact on society. Within thirty years, the Sunday school in England spread to involve 400,000 students.

Some North American churches had organized Sunday classes for the purpose of Bible instruction, although few sought to use lay people in teaching children. Within a few years after the Sunday school began in England, enthusiasm for similar programs quickly spread to North America. Initially the programs were independent of local churches, although they often rented church facilities.

By the 1820s, the Sunday school was spreading rapidly. Most denominations began promoting Sunday schools as a part of the ministry of the local church. The American Sunday School Union was founded and became a major force in the spread of Sunday schools into new areas. As the pioneers moved west, the Sunday school was often the first outpost of Christianity, becoming the nucleus from which churches were later formed. Due in part to the frontier expansion, the Sunday school in North America established itself as a program for all age groups. In England, the dominant pattern continued to involve only children. Many observers believe the American pattern of the all-age Sunday school is one of the keys to the success and health of America's Sunday schools and churches as compared to the health of England's Sunday schools and churches.

Until World War I, the Sunday school saw continuous growth in attendance along with continuous modifications in curriculum and organization. Gradually the Sunday school moved from having the whole school meet together to dividing into groups by ages. Published resources provided instructional plans. A network of conventions provided inspiration and training, often with a high degree of cooperation among denominations. Most important, the Sunday school moved forward due to the dedicated investment of time and energy by a vast number of committed volunteers, most of whom were women.

Between the two world wars, in spite of continued population growth, Sunday schools experienced their first period of decline. Great divisions had developed over vital theological issues. Many denominational leaders no longer held to or promoted the essentials of the faith that were embraced by their church members. With leadership that did not make a priority of either evangelism or Bible teaching, the motivation that had fueled the Sunday school's growth diminished. Momentum was further diminished by controversy that flared over issues of teaching methodology, with many judging one approach or another to reflect a particular theological position.

After World War II, the Sunday school enjoyed a resurgence of interest and growth in evangelical churches. This continued through the 1950s. However, by the 1960s, it was obvious that the Sunday school was struggling. Many churches and their Sunday schools, which had grown rapidly with their communities during the post-war boom years, discovered their numerical increases stopped once the surrounding population stabilized. Congregations became aware that many programs including the Sunday school, which had seemed so successful in attracting new people, had been far more effective in reaching previously churched people than in drawing in the unchurched. When the flow of new people to a community slowed or stopped, in most cases, so did the flow of new people into its churches.

In the years leading up to the sixties, many church leaders were outspoken

Sunday school enthusiasts. By the latter part of the sixties, it was difficult to find a pastor who had anything good to say about the Sunday school. For much of the next two decades, the Sunday school was increasingly seen as a venerable relic that had seen better days and was being replaced by creative new forms. At the same time, the steady increase of women employed outside the home made it more difficult to enlist qualified teachers who were willing and able to invest the time necessary to make their teaching effective.

However, as was pointed out in the introduction to this manual, no other ministry has succeeded in replacing the Sunday school as a widely accepted, effective ministry for outreach and teaching. The Sunday school continues to impact the lives of hundreds of thousands of people every week. Leaders who had relegated the Sunday school to history books have gradually come to realize that the ministry of an effective Sunday school has made many healthy accomplishments in the present and has great potential for the future.

Ministry Goals of the Sunday School

When Robert Raikes began the first Sunday school, he did so to address a significant need. When the Sunday school movement spread across North America, it was also motivated by an important purpose. Sunday school thrived because its teachers understood their mission as vital to the church's reason for being.

One reason for the decline of the Sunday school was a gradual lessening of the sense that the Sunday school was vital and doing something of great importance. In the eyes of many people and in the practice of many churches, Sunday school

became little more than a child care service. The church was expected to provide it, but no one cared about it very deeply. Many church leaders and members seemed to be saying, "It's a good thing for the children of our members, and the adult classes are helpful for the parents and a group of regulars, but I wouldn't want to invest too much time or energy in it."

If your Sunday school is to make a positive impact in the twenty-first century, a commitment must be made to goals that are necessary, worthwhile, and achievable. No one wants to invest time and energy in programs that are not valuable. Who would get excited about a ministry whose reason for being, expressed in one way or another, is to do any of the following:

- Keep the old ship afloat?
- Support our local Sunday school because we've always had one?
- Help out our nice (pastor, Sunday school superintendent, church board, teacher, etc.) because this program is important to him/her?
- Keep the kids occupied while their parents are (in worship, sleeping, eating out, etc.)?
- Keep the parents occupied while their kids . . . ? Oh, you get the idea.

People want to participate in an endeavor that has value. There is no excitement in maintaining the status quo. At the same time, goals that are vague or idealistic discourage people because they never see those goals being reached.

Sunday schools must pursue four highly worthy goals in order to make a positive, lasting impact on people's lives. All four goals are necessary in order to have a balanced, healthful ministry that does not become ingrown or cater only to a narrow segment of people.

Ministry Goal #1:
Win People to Christ

The Sunday school must be committed to reaching people for Christ, both those already a part of a congregation and those who are as yet unchurched.

A Sunday school that is not seeing unchurched people won to Christ is a stagnant program. The greatest damage to the Sunday school's effectiveness occurs when leaders allow it to become ingrown, serving the needs and interests of the faithful while effectively excluding the unchurched. No Sunday school has ever posted a sign announcing, "No Outsiders Allowed," but vast numbers of Sunday schools have operated as though that was their unofficial motto.

A large congregation just completed an attractive new education wing to house children's and youth classes. On the day it opened for use, official signs were posted throughout the building. Refreshments and messy art materials were banned from the rooms. People were warned to keep their hands from marring the walls. A group reaching out to neighborhood young people was restricted from using the building: "We don't want those kids making a mess in here."

One teacher sadly noted the restrictive policies enacted by the church board and said, "I don't think they want real, live kids in this church. I think they're going to end up with a beautiful, empty museum."

Most churches are not so flagrant in erecting barriers to the unchurched. Often the barriers are far more subtle. A couple started attending an adult class while their children received "some good, moral teaching" in their groups down the hall. After several months of sitting quietly, listening to animated discussions about theology and biblical interpretation, they cautiously approached the teacher after a class session.

"How do you like our class?" the teacher asked.

"It's interesting," the wife answered. "But how do you get to know anyone in this group?"

A class that is more interested in its topic than in a visitor is already dying, no matter how lively it may appear.

Is it hard to get teachers who will make a meaningful commitment? Are the few long-term teachers burned out? Seeing people find Christ and become active participants in a group is the single most motivating event in any ministry. Unless a Sunday school sets a goal of winning people to Christ and plans specific strategies to accomplish that goal, the doldrums will set in.

Aren't there other programs that are more effective in evangelism? Why not let the evangelism department or neighborhood Bible studies or Vacation Bible School handle outreach, and let the Sunday school focus on teaching? Besides, unchurched people aren't interested in Sunday school, are they?

Just because a church has some other worthwhile program that focuses on evangelism is no reason for the Sunday school to give up on seeking to win people to Christ. Instead, an outward-looking Sunday school will actively cooperate with evangelism agencies in order to create a welcoming incorporation path for people who are reached through evangelism efforts. If a church's evangelism efforts and its Sunday school operate independently of each other, both programs suffer. When evangelism workers and those they reach are isolated from the rest of the congregation, the Sunday school, especially if it has no outreach efforts of its own, simply stagnates.

The question as to whether unchurched people are interested in attending Sunday school is a little like the question about the chicken and the egg. If a Sunday school has become ingrown and has unintentionally created barriers to outsiders, it will obviously find that outsiders are uninterested in it. But when a Sunday school thoughtfully and intentionally sets out to embrace those on the outside, it discovers many people are open, even willing to respond. Such a result only occurs when a Sunday school sets reaching the unchurched as a major reason for its existence, and then develops and works a plan to accomplish that purpose.

The reproducible worksheet on pages 21 and 22 is helpful for identifying and evaluating current objectives for reaching the unchurched. It is also useful for choosing future actions that will increase attention in this area. Plus, it can help stimulate additional ideas worth pursuing.

Ministry Goal #2: Teach God's Word

A Sunday school must help people both to understand and to apply the truths of God's Word.

Which is more important in Christian teaching—dealing with real-life issues or communicating Bible content?

That question is a little like asking which wing on an airplane is more important—the one on the left or the one on the right? Obviously, if either wing is missing or damaged, the plane will go down.

Similarly, a Sunday school must help people both to understand and apply the truths of God's Word. Otherwise, it falls short of its potential and fails in a crucial part of Christ's instructions to his church.

However, experience shows that teach-ers often fall into one of two common traps that diminish or even eliminate a Sunday school's effectiveness in teaching.

Trap 1: Dealing With Life Issues Independent of Scripture. Under the guise of being relevant, contemporary, or meeting needs, teachers may teach opinions, theories, or facts that may or may not have merit and that lack the underpinning of a solid grounding in Scripture. It is not uncommon for adult and youth classes to explore a variety of topics, giving no more than cursory recognition to biblical insights on those issues. Although contemporary topics can be effectively examined in light of very clear and relevant Scriptures, the great temptation exists for teachers to replace the Bible with psychology, economics, politics, sociology, and other constantly changing sources of "truth."

Trap 2: Teaching Bible Information Unrelated to Life Application. At the other end of the spectrum, while claiming to teach the Bible and while in the very act of dealing with its content, teachers may focus on matters of lesser importance and totally miss the purpose for which the Scriptures were given. It is very possible to fully absorb a class of children in the exciting details of a Bible story without ever exploring the truth God wants to communicate through the narrative. Some teachers become so enamored with fascinating bits of historical, geographical, archaeological, or linguistic trivia, that the clear declaration of God's plan for humanity becomes hopelessly obscured.

Why should the Sunday school in the twenty-first century concern itself with teaching the Bible? We may start looking for our answer in the contemporary problems of human lives. It does not take long to realize that mankind has a deep-seated need that is simply not satisfied apart from the good news revealed in Scripture. Where else can people find guidance direct from our Creator and wisdom that has stood the test of time and crossed all cultural boundaries to bring hope and ultimate meaning to life?

We may start looking in Scripture for a reason to teach the Bible in the modern Sunday school. As we search its pages, we soon realize that, while it deals with history, the Bible is not a history book. It was never intended to be a source for impressive quotes or literary allusions, a cornucopia of facts to be called on in games of Bible trivia. The Bible stands as a record of God's communication to people. Over and over, from Genesis through Revelation, we encounter God speaking. God's reason for speaking was never to share an interesting tidbit of information, to amuse or entertain, or even to pass the time. Not once do we find God "shooting the breeze" with Abraham or David or some crony. God never spoke just to hear his voice echo.

Instead, when God spoke to his people, he clearly stated or obviously implied that his purpose was to instruct them in what they were to do and how they were to live. Every time the Scripture refers to itself, there is no doubt that the message was intended to make a difference in people's lives.

The point of teaching the Bible is not so that people will be able to pass a Bible knowledge quiz or so that they can quote extensive passages of Scripture. The psalmist did not announce (apologies to Psalm 119:11), "I have hidden your word in my heart, that I might get a star on my chart." (The correct ending of that familiar statement is: "That I might not sin against you.") The point of teaching the

Bible, whether in Sunday school or anywhere else, is to guide people in living godly lives, free of the damages inflicted by human willfulness —sin.

The only way to avoid these two traps (dealing with life issues independently of Scripture and teaching Bible information unrelated to life application) is to establish and maintain a teaching approach with a healthful, linked emphasis on both dimensions. Life issues should always be examined in light of Scripture; Scripture should always be studied in terms of what it reveals about life.

The reproducible worksheet on pages 23 and 24 is a helpful tool for identifying and evaluating current directions in teaching God's Word. It is also useful for choosing future actions that will focus attention in this area. Plus, it can help stimulate additional ideas worth pursuing.

Ministry Goal #3: Build Supportive Relationships

The Sunday school and other teaching ministry must be committed to helping build supportive Christian relationships between teachers and learners and among the learners in each group.

I recall sitting among my fellow Primaries, staring uncomfortably at my shoes as my teacher reprimanded me for talking to the boy next to me.

"Wesley!" she announced loud enough for the Juniors and Beginners on the other sides of the partitions to hear. "We do not talk to each other in Sunday school."

I had obviously committed a heinous offense, so our teacher took advantage of this opportunity to expound further on the matter. "We do *not* come to Sunday school to visit with our friends. We come to learn about God."

It took many years for me to realize that

my Sunday school teacher was very, very wrong. I am perfectly willing to admit that I was out of line to have been talking at that moment (not an uncommon fault of mine, as I was often reminded). It is quite possible that my conversation had absolutely nothing to do with what our teacher was trying to get us to learn. However, my seven-year-old chatter was not nearly as wrong as my teacher's pronouncement.

She was right that we come to Sunday school to learn about God. But if there is any place on earth where seven-year-olds, or seventy-year-olds, ought to feel comfortable talking with their friends, it should definitely be the Sunday school. While outreach and Bible instruction are important and worthy goals, in the real world of operating a successful Sunday school, they are very difficult, if not impossible, to achieve unless a third goal is also being accomplished. People are drawn to Sunday school and remain to learn when they are able to establish and deepen meaningful personal relationships.

When asked what they remember most from their years of attendance, adults, who have attended Sunday school all their lives, rarely talk about the lessons that were taught or the facts that were learned. Instead, they talk about a teacher who made a personal impact or friends who were not just fellow learners but were important people in their lives.

Teenagers who drop out of church cite as their major reason for leaving, not a crisis of faith, but simply a desire to be where their friends are. Young people who have not made strong, lasting friendships inside the church are at very high risk to be lost to the church.

Some people interpret this emphasis on relationships as an indictment against the instructional efforts of the Sunday school: "If teachers did a better job of getting their lessons across, people wouldn't be so influenced by others."

Some teachers put up with social requirements as something of a necessary evil: "I have to give my junior high girls time to get all their gabbing out of the way before we can get down to learning something about the Bible."

An emphasis on personal relationships in Sunday school is not a gimmick we use to attract people. It is as valid and essential as an emphasis on outreach and instruction. Far from being a side issue, relationships are at the very core of what the Christian life is all about. If your Sunday school is serious about reaching people for Christ and teaching them to understand and apply God's Word in their lives, your Sunday school must be equally concerned about creating a setting that encourages people to demonstrate and experience the love of Christ in their relationships with one another. The Sunday school must focus on two important types of personal relationships: Teacher/Learner and Learner/Learner.

Teacher/Learner. Henrietta Mears, an influential Christian educator and leader during the first half of the twentieth century, described her own personal pilgrimage, "First I learned to love my teacher. Then I learned to love my teacher's God."

The genius of the Sunday school, in the face of all the ups and downs of more than two centuries, has always been the relationship between a teacher and a relatively small number of learners. In churches of all sizes, the small group structure of Sunday school classes provides an essential opportunity for each person both to be taught and to be cared for by someone "up close."

Unfortunately, many factors get in the way of learners truly learning to love their teacher and then their teacher's God. For example:

- If groups are too large, personal contact is limited, both within class and during the week.
- If teachers change frequently, lasting relationships cannot be built.
- If teachers view their task as only presenting the lesson, they do not invest the time and effort to get to know learners' needs and interests.
- If learners attend sporadically, especially if any of the above factors are also true, relationship-building is hindered.

In contrast, when a Sunday school sees the great value of strong teacher/learner relationships, positive actions can be taken that produce rich benefits for both the teachers and their learners.

Learner/Learner. Over the course of years, even more important than teacher/learner relationships are learner/learner relationships. As children and young people grow, they move from class to class, teacher to teacher. Moving right along with them are their peers. When strong friendships are formed within a class, the potential for godly influence extends into the rest of the week and possibly into future years.

The influence of these friendships can be either positive or negative. Every church has seen friends who supported and encouraged each other to grow in the faith, while other friends have pulled each other away from the church. The challenge facing the Sunday school is to help people of all ages form friendships that support and encourage Christian growth.

The reproducible worksheet on pages 25 and 26 is a helpful tool for identifying

and evaluating current directions in relationship-building. It is also useful for choosing future actions that will focus attention in this area. Plus, it can help stimulate additional ideas worth pursuing.

Ministry Goal #4: Encourage Christian Service

The Sunday school and other teaching ministries must be committed to leading people into active, intentional service to God and others.

During the past generation, some church leaders lost their enthusiasm for the Sunday school due to the far too frequent pattern of classes becoming stagnant. Groups that had been together for years became ingrown, enjoying interesting teaching and their own fellowship. These Sunday school classes became the spiritual equivalents of the Dead Sea—always taking in, never giving out until all signs of life were extinguished.

A basic law of the Christian life and of an effective teaching ministry is that people who receive must also give. That giving must be for the benefit of others, not ourselves. Consider the following examples:

- Children are told that the money they put in the offering is used to pay for Sunday school books and supplies, or for the electric bill, or custodial services. While those are worthwhile and even necessary expenditures, the children are the beneficiaries of their own giving. Until they are led to give or serve to benefit someone else, they may be learning responsibility, but they have not learned generosity.
- An adult claims he cannot get involved in leading, teaching, or helping in Sunday school because he needs the

fine teaching he enjoys in his class. While there are times in everyone's life when the need to receive is vital, when that need becomes a continuing pattern and an excuse not to give, Christian growth is seriously stunted.

When a Sunday school consistently emphasizes reaching out to unchurched people, learning and applying God's Word, and building supportive relationships, an emphasis on personal involvement in Christian service is a natural, but not automatic, outgrowth. Human nature has always found it too easy to listen to God's truth, to nod assent to his message, but then to do nothing about it. Even the great heroes of Scripture were reluctant to leave their familiar patterns of life and risk doing what God called them to do. An effective Sunday school will recognize this common tendency and carefully plan ways to encourage people to get involved in active service individually and corporately.

The reproducible worksheet on pages 27-30 is a helpful tool for identifying and evaluating current directions in leading people into Christian service. It is also useful for choosing future actions that will focus attention in this area. Plus, it can help stimulate additional ideas worth pursuing.

Can Your Sunday School Be Effective?

Perhaps the four worksheets in this chapter caused you to feel overwhelmed because of the enormous amount of work involved in running an effective Sunday school. Such a feeling is certainly justified, for building and maintaining a ministry that is reaching out to new people, teaching the Bible effectively, building positive relationships, and guiding people into active service is a big job—a very big job. In fact, there simply is no job anywhere that is any bigger!

Early in my own ministry I was feeling overwhelmed with just how big that job is. I thought I was floundering in my efforts to improve our Sunday school. A layman from another church, who was responsible for far more than I was, shared some old, simple, but very true advice: The key to succeeding is to plan your work; then work your plan.

He was right. At that point in my ministry, I was working very hard, but I had no real plan. I was running from one problem to another, not moving myself or anyone else in a consistent, productive direction.

On the other hand, I've also seen and worked with leaders who were enamored with planning. They expended all their time and energy in committee meetings, devising massive handbooks filled with charts and other impressive goodies. By the time the plan was ready, everyone involved was worn out and the plan was never really worked.

There is no way any Sunday school can effectively implement all the sample strategies on the four worksheets in this chapter. But any Sunday school that prayerfully focuses on a few objectives at a time will soon see progress. In many cases, it is best to begin by targeting one age level (usually the one where the current staff is most open to improvements), then choosing the goals, objectives, and strategies to pursue.

Once you have a few successes under your belt, your faith will grow that God can use you to improve your Sunday school. At the same time, your credibility as a leader will grow with those you work alongside. That will make the next round of objectives easier to achieve.

MINISTRY GOAL #1:
Win People to Christ

Three related terms are used on this sheet.

Goals are broad statements of intent. They are declarations of the major, long-term emphases desired for ministry efforts.

Objectives are more focused, short-term statements that can be used to measure progress toward a goal.

Strategies are planned actions intended to accomplish an objective.

Mark the actions to rate your present and planned efforts for winning people to Christ. Focus on specific age groups or the whole school. Space is provided for additional goals, objectives, and strategies.

E=Excellent
S=Satisfactorily
   Doing Now
I=Improvement Needed
N=Need to Start

EC=Early Childhood
C=Children
Y=Youth
A=Adult

Goals

1. We have a clear statement declaring that reaching people for Christ is a major purpose of our ministry.

   Sample Statement: *The Sunday school is committed to reaching people for Christ, both those already a part of our congregation and those who are as yet unchurched.*

2. Current church and Sunday school leaders are on record agreeing with and supporting this statement.

EC	C	Y	A

3. Current Sunday school staff members are regularly made aware of this statement.

EC	C	Y	A

4. All plans and activities of the Sunday school are evaluated in light of their contribution to fulfilling this statement.

EC	C	Y	A

5. _____

   _____

EC	C	Y	A

Objectives

1. We have realistic and challenging numerical goals that measure progress in outreach efforts. We have set goals for the following:

   • the number of prospects invited

EC	C	Y	A

   • the number of first time visitors

EC	C	Y	A

Three related terms are used on this sheet.

Goals are broad statements of intent. They are declarations of the major, long-term emphases desired for ministry efforts.

Objectives are more focused, short-term statements that can be used to measure progress toward a goal.

Strategies are planned actions intended to accomplish an objective.

Mark the actions to rate your present and planned efforts for winning people to Christ. Focus on specific age groups or the whole school. Space is provided for additional goals, objectives, and strategies.

E=Excellent
S=Satisfactorily Doing Now
I=Improvement Needed
N=Need to Start

EC=Early Childhood
C=Children
Y=Youth
A=Adult

MINISTRY GOAL #1:
Win People to Christ
2

- the number of prospect and visitor contacts made

EC	C	Y	A

- the number of new converts and/or enrolled attenders

EC	C	Y	A

- total attendance growth

EC	C	Y	A

- _____

EC	C	Y	A

2. _____

_____

EC	C	Y	A

Strategies

1. All Sunday school staff members attend one or more training sessions designed to equip them to reach out to new people, to build relationships with those who have been reached, and to present clearly the essential truths about becoming a Christian.

EC	C	Y	A

2. All Sunday school staff members participate in efforts to develop and implement plans for reaching out to the unchurched and to those within the congregation who are not presently involved in Sunday school. (*See Chapter 2 for outreach ideas.*)

EC	C	Y	A

3. _____

_____

EC	C	Y	A

MINISTRY GOAL #2:
Teach God's Word

Three related terms are used on this sheet.

Goals are broad statements of intent. They are declarations of the major, long-term emphases desired for ministry efforts.

Objectives are more focused, short-term statements that can be used to measure progress toward a goal.

Strategies are planned actions intended to accomplish an objective.

Mark the actions to rate your present and planned efforts for teaching God's Word. Focus on specific age groups or the whole school. Space is provided for additional goals, objectives, and strategies.

E=Excellent
S=Satisfactorily
　　Doing Now
I=Improvement Needed
N=Need to Start

EC=Early Childhood
C=Children
Y=Youth
A=Adult

MINISTRY GOAL #2:
Teach God's Word
1

Goals

1. We have a clear statement declaring that teaching people both to understand and to apply God's Word is a major purpose of our ministry. ____

   Sample Statement: *The Sunday school is committed to teaching people to both understand and apply the truths of God's Word.*

2. Current church and Sunday school leaders are on record agreeing with and supporting this statement.

   ‾‾EC‾‾　‾‾C‾‾　‾‾Y‾‾　‾‾A‾‾

3. Current Sunday school staff members are regularly made aware of this statement.

   ‾‾EC‾‾　‾‾C‾‾　‾‾Y‾‾　‾‾A‾‾

4. All teaching efforts of the Sunday school are evaluated in light of their contribution to fulfilling this statement.

   ‾‾EC‾‾　‾‾C‾‾　‾‾Y‾‾　‾‾A‾‾

5. _____

   _____

   ‾‾EC‾‾　‾‾C‾‾　‾‾Y‾‾　‾‾A‾‾

Objectives

We have realistic and challenging goals that measure progress in instructional efforts.

1. We regularly invest a stated dollar amount to improve curriculum and other resources available to aid teachers in effective Bible instruction.

   ‾‾EC‾‾　‾‾C‾‾　‾‾Y‾‾　‾‾A‾‾

2. We evaluate the teaching efforts of a stated number of teachers each month.

   ‾‾EC‾‾　‾‾C‾‾　‾‾Y‾‾　‾‾A‾‾

3. We provide at least a minimum amount of training in instructional procedures for at least a stated percentage of the total staff.

| EC | C | Y | A |

4. We make improvements and do maintenance work that aids the teaching/learning process in the facilities of at least one department or classroom each quarter.

5. _____

_____

| EC | C | Y | A |

Three related terms are used on this sheet.

Goals are broad statements of intent. They are declarations of the major, long-term emphases desired for ministry efforts.

Objectives are more focused, short-term statements that can be used to measure progress toward a goal.

Strategies are planned actions intended to accomplish an objective.

Mark the actions to rate your present and planned efforts for teaching God's Word. Focus on specific age groups or the whole school. Space is provided for additional goals, objectives, and strategies.

E=Excellent
S=Satisfactorily
 Doing Now
I=Improvement Needed
N=Need to Start

EC=Early Childhood
C=Children
Y=Youth
A=Adult

Strategies

1. We choose curriculum resources that effectively aid teachers and learners of all age groups in understanding biblical truth and applying it in daily living.

| EC | C | Y | A |

2. All Sunday school staff members attend one or more training sessions designed to equip them to use their curriculum resources effectively.

| EC | C | Y | A |

3. We observe the teaching procedures presently being used by all staff members, affirming positive efforts and developing plans to improve where needed.

| EC | C | Y | A |

4. All Sunday school staff members participate in efforts to develop and implement plans for improving teaching procedures. (See Chapter 3 for an overview of age level appropriate instructional plans.)

| EC | C | Y | A |

5. We evaluate facilities to identify potential hindrances (e.g., distractions, crowding, inadequate storage) to effective teaching and learning. (See Chapter 8 for detailed facility guidance.)

| EC | C | Y | A |

6. _____

_____

| EC | C | Y | A |

MINISTRY GOAL #2:
Teach God's Word
2

MINISTRY GOAL #3:
Build Supportive Relationships

Three related terms are used on this sheet.

Goals are broad statements of intent. They are declarations of the major, long-term emphases desired for ministry efforts.

Objectives are more focused, short-term statements that can be used to measure progress toward a goal.

Strategies are planned actions intended to accomplish an objective.

Mark the actions to rate your present and planned efforts for building supportive relationships. Focus on specific age groups or the whole school. Space is provided for additional goals, objectives, and strategies.

E=Excellent
S=Satisfactorily
    Doing Now
I=Improvement Needed
N=Need to Start

EC=Early Childhood
C=Children
Y=Youth
A=Adult

MINISTRY GOAL #3
Build Supportive Relationships
1

Goals

1. We have a clear statement declaring that building supportive relationships is a major purpose of our ministry. ____

   Sample Statement: The Sunday school is committed to helping build supportive Christian relationships between teachers and learners and among the learners in each group.

2. Current church and Sunday school leaders are on record agreeing with and supporting this statement.

EC	C	Y	A

3. Current Sunday school staff members are regularly made aware of this statement.

EC	C	Y	A

4. All teaching efforts of the Sunday school are evaluated in light of their contribution to fulfilling this statement.

EC	C	Y	A

5. _____

   _____

EC	C	Y	A

Objectives

We have realistic and challenging goals that measure progress in efforts to encourage relationship-building.

1. We maintain group sizes and teacher-to-learner ratios that enable teachers and learners to get to know one another well. (See Chapter 4 for grouping and ratios information.)

EC	C	Y	A

2. We maintain an administrative structure that enables leaders to build supportive relationships with teachers. (See Chapter 6 for administrative guidelines.)

EC	C	Y	A

3. We provide at least a minimum amount of training in relationship-building skills for at least a stated percentage of the total staff.

EC	C	Y	A

4. We conduct a stated number of relationship-building events each quarter or year.

EC	C	Y	A

5. _____

_____

EC	C	Y	A

Strategies

1. All Sunday school staff members attend one or more training sessions designed to equip them to build relationships both inside and outside of class, emphasizing both teacher/learner and learner/learner relationships.

EC	C	Y	A

2. We provide Sunday school staff with a variety of relationship-building ideas to use in class and during the week.

EC	C	Y	A

3. We observe the current relationship-building efforts of all Sunday school staff members, affirming positive efforts and developing plans to improve where needed.

EC	C	Y	A

4. _____

_____

EC	C	Y	A

Three related terms are used on this sheet.

Goals are broad statements of intent. They are declarations of the major, long-term emphases desired for ministry efforts.

Objectives are more focused, short-term statements that can be used to measure progress toward a goal.

Strategies are planned actions intended to accomplish an objective.

Mark the actions to rate your present and planned efforts for building supportive relationships. Focus on specific age groups or the whole school. Space is provided for additional goals, objectives, and strategies.

E=Excellent
S=Satisfactorily Doing Now
I=Improvement Needed
N=Need to Start

EC=Early Childhood
C=Children
Y=Youth
A=Adult

MINISTRY GOAL #3
Build Supportive Relationships
2

MINISTRY GOAL #4:
Encourage Christian Service

Three related terms are used on this sheet.

Goals are broad statements of intent. They are declarations of the major, long-term emphases desired for ministry efforts.

Objectives are more focused, short-term statements that can be used to measure progress toward a goal.

Strategies are planned actions intended to accomplish an objective.

Mark the actions to rate your present and planned efforts for encouraging Christian service. Focus on specific age groups or the whole school. Space is provided for additional goals, objectives, and strategies.

E=Excellent
S=Satisfactorily Doing Now
I=Improvement Needed
N=Need to Start

EC=Early Childhood
C=Children
Y=Youth
A=Adult

MINISTRY GOAL #4
Encourage Christian Service
1

Goals

1. We have a clear statement declaring that leading people into active Christian service is a major purpose of our ministry.

   Sample Statement: *The Sunday school is committed to leading people into active, intentional service to God and others.*

2. Current church and Sunday school leaders are on record agreeing with and supporting this statement.

EC	C	Y	A

3. Current Sunday school staff members are regularly made aware of this statement.

EC	C	Y	A

4. All teaching efforts of the Sunday school are evaluated in light of their contribution to fulfilling this statement.

EC	C	Y	A

5. _____

   _____

EC	C	Y	A

Strategies

1. We conduct a brainstorming session for all Sunday school staff seeking to identify a wide variety of possible service opportunities for individuals and groups in each age level.

EC	C	Y	A

2. We help Sunday school staff members link Bible-learning emphases with ministry opportunities throughout the congregation.

EC	C	Y	A

3. We provide all adult groups with lists or posters identifying current or past members who are serving elsewhere.

EC   C   Y   A

4. We recognize or reward the adult/youth teacher or leader whose group contributes the most people to service with other groups.

EC   C   Y   A

5. We report to the congregation on service projects undertaken by specific classes.

EC   C   Y   A

6. _____

_____

EC   C   Y   A

Objectives

We have realistic and challenging goals that measure progress in efforts to involve people in active Christian service. For example:

1. We regularly present age-level appropriate service project opportunities to all classes, such as:

   • Provide refreshments for another church group.

EC   C   Y   A

   • Raise money for a local or foreign mission project.

EC   C   Y   A

   • Assist at a rescue mission or homeless shelter.

EC   C   Y   A

   • Donate new/used items for a community or mission agency.

EC   C   Y   A

   • Present a program (e.g., music, Scripture) at a retirement or nursing home.

EC   C   Y   A

Three related terms are used on this sheet.

Goals are broad statements of intent. They are declarations of the major, long-term emphases desired for ministry efforts.

Objectives are more focused, short-term statements that can be used to measure progress toward a goal.

Strategies are planned actions intended to accomplish an objective.

Mark the actions to rate your present and planned efforts for encouraging Christian service. Focus on specific age groups or the whole school. Space is provided for additional goals, objectives, and strategies.

E=Excellent
S=Satisfactorily Doing Now
I=Improvement Needed
N=Need to Start

EC=Early Childhood
C=Children
Y=Youth
A=Adult

MINISTRY GOAL #4
Encourage Christian Service
2

• Organize a work party at the church building, at another church, at a community or mission agency, or at someone's home.

EC	C	Y	A

Three related terms are used on this sheet.

Goals are broad statements of intent. They are declarations of the major, long-term emphases desired for ministry efforts.

Objectives are more focused, short-term statements that can be used to measure progress toward a goal.

Strategies are planned actions intended to accomplish an objective.

Mark the actions to rate your present and planned efforts for encouraging Christian service. Focus on specific age groups or the whole school. Space is provided for additional goals, objectives, and strategies.

E=Excellent
S=Satisfactorily
 Doing Now
I=Improvement Needed
N=Need to Start

EC=Early Childhood
C=Children
Y=Youth
A=Adult

• Collect canned/packaged food for needy families or for a food pantry.

EC	C	Y	A

• Form a prayer chain to intercede when needs arise.

EC	C	Y	A

• _____

EC	C	Y	A

2. We enlist a stated number of individuals from each class for service opportunities, such as:

Early Childhood and Children (may need adult assistance)

• Invite a friend to a church or family event.

EC	C

• Pick up litter on church grounds and in neighborhood.

EC	C

• Accompany a teacher to visit an absentee or visitor.

EC	C

• Write letters to college students, missionaries, military personnel, and so on.

EC	C

• _____

EC	C

• _____

EC	C

Three related terms are used on this sheet.

Goals are broad statements of intent. They are declarations of the major, long-term emphases desired for ministry efforts.
Objectives are more focused, short-term statements that can be used to measure progress toward a goal.
Strategies are planned actions intended to accomplish an objective.

Mark the actions to rate your present and planned efforts for encouraging Christian service. Focus on specific age groups or the whole school. Space is provided for additional goals, objectives, and strategies.

E=Excellent
S=Satisfactorily
   Doing Now
I=Improvement Needed
N=Need to Start

EC=Early Childhood
  C=Children
  Y=Youth
  A=Adult

MINISTRY GOAL #4
Encourage Christian Service
4

Youth and Adult

- Lead, teach, or help in Sunday school classes or other teaching ministries.

        Y   A

- Visit shut-ins.

        Y   A

- Provide child care for families needing assistance.

        Y   A

- Write letters to college students, missionaries, military personnel, and so on.

        Y   A

- Provide at-home assistance (gardening, painting, plumbing repairs, meals, etc.) for families or singles in need.

        Y   A

- Tutor students needing help with school work.

        Y   A

- _____

  _____

        Y   A

- _____

  _____

        Y   A

3. _____

  _____

        Y   A

2
Reaching People

I was leading a workshop for Christian education leaders. I shared some ideas for generating excitement in the Sunday school in order to attract people and effectively challenge them in growth. I thought the administrators in the room were responding positively to the various tips and suggestions and even to a few gimmicks I tossed in. When I assigned them to work in groups to share some promotional ideas they had used, there was a great deal of animated discussion. So, when I invited the groups to share their best ideas, I was pleased when a woman quickly raised her hand. (What teacher doesn't enjoy the quick responses of eager learners?)

Smiling expectantly, I called on the woman to share one of her group's ideas.

"I think this whole topic is a waste of our time," she began.

I kept smiling and began to nod my head affirmatively, which was clear evidence that I am not always quick on the uptake. She continued, evidently accepting my smile and nods as agreement.

"All of this emphasis on promotion and publicity, on trying to arouse interest, and on motivating people is totally inappropriate for Sunday school leaders," she said without pausing for a breath or giving me a chance to stop nodding or smiling. "We're educators," she declared, "not promoters!"

Suddenly, her point registered. I'm not sure exactly what happened next as my brain tried to shift out of its eager, happy learner mode. I wish I could be certain that I adroitly recovered my balance, affirming the woman for expressing her concerns. I wish I could remember brilliantly presenting a host of unassailable

31

reasons that caused the woman to recognize clearly the great value of promoting the Sunday school. Unfortunately, the only mental image I can recall of what happened next involves me babbling while the woman continued to look at me with suspicion until the workshop ended and we all went home.

Educators and Promoters

There was probably a good reason why that woman was reluctant to see her role as a promoter. After all, the word promoter has been associated with hucksters and flacks and carnival barkers. Surely the educational ministry of the church deserves, even requires, a better term.

Promoter is actually a very good word because it describes an essential aspect of the job of leading an educational ministry.

Must the effective Sunday school leader be both a teacher and a booster, an instructor and a motivator, a promoter and an educator? These questions are asked frequently among ministry leaders, and they probe the heart of what makes an effective Sunday school. In an ideal world, everyone would recognize the great value of attending Sunday school. After informing people about the time and place that groups meet, the crowds would all arrive, ready and eager to learn.

However, in this less than perfect world of ours, both inside and outside the church, people who need Christian instruction, nurture, and fellowship stay away from Sunday school.

Leaders who succeed in guiding effective, growing ministries are those who give a significant amount of attention to *both* the quality of the learning experiences and the actions that inform and attract people to participate in those experiences.

If we are to succeed, we must focus our attention on outreach. And if we are to reach people, we must be both educators and promoters.

Target Your Audience: Define Your Market

Jesus was often criticized because he spent time and energy reaching out to sinners. Jesus forcefully defended his actions and established a pattern we too often forget to follow. When asked why he spent time with sinners, Jesus answered, "It is not the healthy who need a doctor, but the sick. I have not come to call the righteous, but sinners to repentance."

Jesus knew whom he was trying to reach; and he reached them.

Unfortunately, many Sunday schools do not have a vision for whom they might reach. They have empty chairs stacked against the wall or in closets, but they have no clear idea of who the people are who could fill them. As a result, years go by, the chairs remain empty, and leaders wonder why the people haven't come.

Who Are the People in Your Community?

New churches tend to grow more rapidly than established churches. One reason for this growth is because the people who establish new churches focus on their community. They seek to discover all they can about who lives and works there and what needs and concerns exist. The people involved in a new church are aware that the whole point of launching a new church is to minister to the people of the surrounding area.

In contrast, many established churches are more focused on existing programs and the people who already attend. This leaves little time and energy to take a fresh look at their neighborhoods. As a result, it does not take long for ethnic, age, family, and economic changes to occur, often leaving a church out of touch with the very people whom they should be reaching.

The reproducible worksheet on pages 37 and 38 is a helpful tool for identifying and evaluating current efforts for reaching unchurched people for Christ. It is also useful for choosing future actions that will increase attention in this area. Plus, it can help stimulate additional ideas worth pursuing.

Who Are the People in Your Congregation?

Just as leaders must learn all they can about the community they are seeking to impact, so must they know the people within the congregation who are not currently involved in an educational ministry. Some leaders simply dismiss these people as not interested or too busy, or some variation of uncommitted, unspiritual, or fringe people. Other leaders assume that those who do not attend Sunday school (or some other instructional program) have been given many opportunities to attend and just aren't the type to respond. Once a label has been applied, it no longer seems as urgent to make efforts to draw these people into active participation in a class or group.

Within every congregation are people who would both benefit from and enjoy participation in a Christian education ministry. These people include:

- Children whose parents don't seem to care enough to bring them;
- Parents who feel guilty about having their child participate in a program for

which they aren't prepared to volunteer;
- Teens who lack strong friendships in the group and either feel uncomfortable attending or prefer to go where their friends are;
- Seniors whose health makes regular attendance difficult or who find it difficult to sit through both Sunday school and a worship service;
- People who just don't feel they fit in the groups being offered.

A church that takes seriously the responsibility to reach people must find and help those who do not automatically participate in the present church programs.

The reproducible worksheet on pages 39 and 40 is a helpful tool for identifying and evaluating current efforts for reaching people who are a part of the congregation but do not participate in current teaching ministries. It is also useful for choosing future actions that will increase attention in this area. Plus, it can help stimulate additional ideas worth pursuing.

Who Is Responsible for Outreach Efforts?

Experience has taught us that what is everyone's job is often no one's job. Many churches fail to reach out because no one has been given the primary responsibility for outreach.

At the same time, experience has also taught us that what I perceive as your job is probably not going to be seen as my job. Many churches fail to reach out because outreach has become the job of an elite few on the evangelism or outreach committee.

To make outreach an ongoing and effective part of a church's educational ministries, someone (actually a group of someones) needs to assume that responsibility. These people are not responsible to do all the outreach-related work. Their responsibility is to set the pace and lead the rest of the staff in outreach functions.

Enlist an **outreach director** for your educational ministries, someone with a deep concern for those who need to be reached. This person makes sure that the goal of reaching new people remains a top priority in everything that gets done. Some actions the outreach director can take include:

1. Enlist an **outreach leader** for each program and/or department to work with those staff members in their outreach efforts.
2. Promote outreach objectives with all staff members.
3. Encourage and assist staff members in outreach efforts (e.g., visitor follow-up, encouraging members to invite unchurched friends, planning events with appeal to the unchurched).
4. Ensure that accurate records are kept so that contacts with visitors and prospects can be effectively maintained.
5. Cooperate with the church's outreach efforts to build effective bridges for people reached through those endeavors.

Organize for Growth

Far too many educational ministries and the churches that sponsor them fail to grow because they fail to organize themselves with growth in mind. They assume they don't need to change. The church retains structures and procedures that work at one size but not the next.

Here are the most common organizational changes that will encourage and sustain outreach and growth: Increase space, add staff, create new groups, and expand administrative support.

Increase Space

Groups that are crowded or even comfortable have very little incentive to seek more people. These groups make it more difficult to incorporate new people if they do visit. In adult and youth groups, crowded rooms inhibit people from making the effort to meet and converse with a new person who is on the other side of the room. In children's groups, crowding discourages teachers from following up on visitors and absentees, let alone seeking to reach new prospects.

Add Staff

The teacher-to-learner ratios in the above chart encourage teachers and leaders to consistently engage in the necessary efforts to build attendance. If the number of learners per teacher exceeds the recommended ratios, outreach efforts will be sporadic.

The church that wants to grow by reaching out to new people must plan ahead, adding staff *before* groups become unwieldy and outreach efforts have decreased. This can be done in one of two ways, depending on whether the new staff person will work in an existing group or will form a new group.

Add staff within an existing group. As soon as the number of learners in a group approaches the recommended ratios, a new teacher should be enlisted. For a period of time, this new person should observe and assist other teachers and should also work in ongoing outreach efforts. As soon as possible, the new teacher should be assigned a group of learners to be his/her own class or small group.

Add staff to start a new group. When starting a new department or class that will meet separately from the existing group, decide first whether any of the current staff will move to the new group or whether a totally new teaching team will be enlisted. (*See "Create New Groups" below.*)

- Assigning some of the current staff to the new group ensures a degree of experience in the new group. In this case, enlist the new staff member to work for a period of time in the existing group before starting the new group.
- However, if the new staff will operate with significant changes from the way the existing staff operates, start the new group with fresh leadership. In this case, the new staff must be prepared so they are ready to take over at the first meeting of the new group. An experienced leader may be enlisted to assist the new staff for several months until they are ready to "solo."

(*See Chapter 7 for help with recruiting and training new staff.*)

Create New Groups

A church that wants to grow by reaching out to new people must regularly create new groups to give impetus to that growth. A new group should be started whenever an existing group approaches the maximum attendance listed in the "Recommended Space and Staff Allotments" chart on page 41.

Talk about *starting* a new group rather than *dividing* an existing one. People are threatened when hearing that their beloved group is going to be split. Starting a new group is seen as a positive step forward. While this may seem like an exercise in semantics, the attitude people have about a change is important to how well the change will succeed.

(*See Chapter 4 for further information on creating new groups.*)

Expand Administrative Support

As attendance grows—and often in order for growth to occur—changes need to be made in administrative structures. For example, in a small Sunday school, it may be possible for one general superintendent to provide effective leadership for all groups. That effectiveness will diminish with each additional teacher or group. Ultimately, attendance and growth will plateau largely due to the superintendent's inability to provide effective leadership.

One of the first additional leadership roles to add in order to stimulate and maintain growth is the outreach director mentioned earlier in this chapter.

Vital administrative positions to add include department leaders (whenever three or more teachers are working with an age level) and age level coordinators (whenever an age division has three or more department leaders).

(*See Chapter 6 for information on administrative responsibilities. Note the discussion on "Range of Relationships" in the "Manage Operations" section near the end of that chapter.*)

Reaching People in the Community

Mark the actions to rate your present and planned efforts for reaching unchurched people for Christ. Space is provided for additional ideas for reaching the unchurched.

E=Excellent
S=Satisfactorily
    Doing Now
I=Improvement Needed
N=Need to Start

Identify prospects.

____ 1. Encourage members to choose an unchurched friend or family member to invite.

____ 2. Secure information on members' friends and family to invite.

____ 3. Secure information on visitors and others who have attended church services or other events or who have been contacted in the church's outreach efforts.

____ 4. Identify community demographics (age ranges, family status, ethnic groupings, economic levels, length of residence, etc.).

____ 5. Survey (phone or door-to-door) specific neighborhoods.

____ 6. Select target group or groups for whom to focus ministry efforts.

____ 7. _____

_____

Motivate and equip staff and members to reach out to the unchurched.

____ 1. Plan all group activities in terms of how an unchurched person would view them.

____ 2. Regularly encourage staff and members to pray for and invite unchurched friends and family.

____ 3. Regularly share age-level appropriate experiences of those who have reached out to unchurched friends or family.

____ 4. Regularly present age-level appropriate instruction to staff and members on how to reach out to the unchurched. Include the following:

    ____ How to build friendships by showing Christian love;

    ____ How to invite someone to a church event;

    ____ How to share your faith.

____ _____

___ 5. _____

_____

Mark the actions to rate your present and planned efforts for reaching unchurched people for Christ. Space is provided for additional ideas for reaching the unchurched.

E=Excellent
S=Satisfactorily Doing Now
I=Improvement Needed
N=Need to Start

Actively seek the participation of unchurched prospects.

___ 1. Plan periodic events and topics designed specifically to attract unchurched friends and family.

___ 2. Conduct planned efforts to contact prospects (e.g., by mail, by phone, in person).

___ 3. Plan and carry out friendly follow-up contacts to new and repeat visitors.

___ 4. _____

_____

Clearly and attractively present opportunities to receive Christ.

___ 1. Select curriculum resources that encourage and assist leaders to present information on receiving Christ.

___ 2. Encourage staff and members in age-appropriate contacts to share their faith with family and friends who have attended.

___ 3. _____

_____

Intentionally follow up on individuals who receive Christ.

___ 1. Choose age-appropriate materials to provide to new Christians.

___ 2. Assign a mature Christian (staff or member) to personally follow up with a new Christian.

___ 3. Encourage staff and members to incorporate a new Christian into full life of a group.

___ 4. _____

_____

Reaching People Within the Congregation

Mark the actions to rate your present and planned efforts for reaching people within your congregation. Space is provided for additional ideas for reaching people within your congregation.

E=Excellent
S=Satisfactorily Doing Now
I=Improvement Needed
N=Need to Start

Identify people in the congregation who do not attend Sunday school or other educational ministries.

____ 1. Compare Sunday school and other group rosters with membership and worship attendance lists to identify those who do not participate in an educational ministry.

____ 2. Enlist teachers, leaders, and participants of teaching ministries to identify people they know who are part of the church family but do not participate in a educational ministry.

____ 3. _____

_____

Discover reasons why these people do not attend educational ministries.

____ 1. Mail a survey form, stating a desire to better meet needs of the total congregation. Invite people to indicate why they do not now attend and under what circumstances they would attend. (A multiple choice survey is easiest for people to complete, but should allow ample space for people to add comments or additional explanations.) Be prepared to follow up with at least one additional mailing or telephone call to get people to complete and turn in survey forms.

____ 2. Conduct phone interviews with nonattenders, asking their help in improving church ministries.

____ 3. Conduct in-person interviews with nonattenders, asking their help in improving church ministries.

___ 4. _____

_____

Mark the actions to rate your present and planned efforts for reaching people within your congregation. Space is provided for additional ideas for reaching people within your congregation.

E=Excellent
S=Satisfactorily
    Doing Now
I=Improvement Needed
N=Need to Start

Explore possible program changes in light of the surveys and interviews.

___ 1. Are there individuals or groups whose needs are not met by current groups? Do new groups need to be created? (People who have knowingly not been attending a group are more likely to begin attending a new group than to attend the group they have previously rejected.)

___ 2. Do present procedures of current groups need to be modified to attract and welcome those who do not now attend?

___ 3. What types of communication (e.g., mail, phone calls, bulletin announcements, personal contacts) would best reach these people and successfully encourage their attendance?

___ 4. _____

_____

Recommended Space and Staff Allotments

Age Group	Space Per Person	Maximum Attendance	Room Size	Teacher: Learner Ratio
Early Childhood				
Ages 0-12 mo.	35 sq. ft.	15	600-900 sq. ft.	1:2
Ages 12-24 mo.	35 sq. ft.	15	600-900 sq. ft.	1:2
Ages 2-3 years	35 sq. ft.	16	700-900 sq. ft.	1:3
Ages 4-6 years	35 sq. ft.	20	800-900 sq. ft.	1:4
Children				
Grades 1-2	30 sq. ft.	25	800-900 sq. ft.	1:6
Grades 3-6	30 sq. ft.	30	900 sq. ft.	1:8
Youth				
Grades 6-12	25 sq. ft.	40	900-1000 sq. ft.	1:8
Adult				
Ages 18+	15 sq. ft.	40	600-900 sq. ft.	1:8*

* The adult ratio indicates the number of people per group leader for care groups established within larger classes or small groups that meet independently.

A good rule of thumb in the early childhood division is to match the teacher-to-learner ratio to the age of the child. For example, provide one worker for every two two-year-olds, for every three three-year-olds, etc.

Standard size rooms (i.e., 800-900 sq. ft.; 24' x 36') are the most efficient room sizes; they allow a variety of seating arrangements and can be used with minimal modification for any age group as a church's needs change.

(See Chapter 8 for further guidelines on space and facilities. See Chapter 4 for further information on group sizes and ratios.)

3
Teaching and Learning Strategies

Good teaching does not just happen. Good teaching is not something that a church either has or does not have. If a church lacks the skills that good teaching requires, something can be done to acquire them.

Good teaching in the life of a church is the result of an intentional, coordinated plan. Good teaching grows out of a common awareness among leaders and the congregation that an effective church must be a teaching church.

While the basic principles of learning apply to people of all ages, some differences occur in the ways those principles are implemented. Learning at any age is the process not just of acquisition but also of application. When have I learned Ephesians 4:32: "Be kind to one another"? Have I learned it when I have heard it or repeated it? Have I learned it when I have memorized it or given examples that show

that I understand it? Not until I have shown kindness in my attitudes and actions can I claim to have learned those five words. When dealing with the truths of God's Word, learning must always lead to growth, to changes in understanding, attitudes, and actions.

Learning by Doing

"People learn by doing" is an oft-repeated truism in education. The statement recognizes that we are more likely to understand and remember the things we have actually done rather than the things we have merely heard about. But just because students are busy doing things does not necessarily mean they are learning what the teacher intended. In many cases, the real learning that results from a student's activity is almost totally unrelated to the desired outcome.

- A group of adults during a lecture may or may not be learning what the lecturer is saying, but they are learning to sit quietly and look interested.
- Teenagers answering questions may or may not be learning the subject on which they are being quizzed, but they are learning to give answers acceptable to the teacher and/or group.
- Children drawing pictures of a Bible story may or may not be learning about the story, but they are learning to express their ideas visually.

The challenge for the teacher is to find ways to involve learners in some form of doing—mental, verbal, social, physical—so that what students do is closely related to what the teacher wants them to learn. While all people learn by doing, the kinds of doing are not the same for two-year-olds as for twelve-year-olds, or twenty-year-olds, or eighty-two-year-olds.

However, it would be a mistake, as well, to assume that a two-year-old learns in exactly the same manner as all other two-year-olds, or that all eighty-two-year-olds are identical in their approaches to learning. Within any group of children, teens, or adults, a wide diversity will exist in learning approaches. Some researchers have focused on distinct learning styles, noting that some people learn better through one means, while others learn better through another. In addition, in any group differences exist in intelligence, background, previous knowledge, life needs, attention spans, reading ability, and interests. The challenge, therefore, is not to find one method that every teacher should use, but to develop balanced approaches that accommodate the fascinating diversity of people.

Thus, this chapter explores effective methods and procedures of guiding balanced learning experiences for groups in four major age divisions:

- Early Childhood (Birth-Age 6)
- Children (Grades 1-6)
- Youth (Grades 6-12)
- Adults (Ages 18 and up)

These divisions recognize that not all churches group children and young people the same way. Thus, there is a measure of overlap between these divisions. In situations that include learners from two of these divisions (e.g., a children's church for four-year-olds through third grade), leaders must emphasize elements that are appropriate for children in both divisions, minimizing use of elements that fit only children in one division (i.e., reading skills that the younger children do not have).

Early Childhood (Birth—Age 6)

The most obvious characteristic of young children is that, if they are awake, they are probably moving. Effective teachers of young children who respect the Creator's plan of maturation will provide many opportunities for purposeful movement, keeping "sit still and be quiet" times to a minimum.

The church that sets a goal of teaching God's Word in such a way that people will apply its truths in daily living finds that a good program for young children provides many opportunities to put learning into practice right on the spot. More than just talking about applying truth, the activity-based early childhood classroom is filled with "teachable moments" when children are actually living out what they learn from Bible verses, stories, and songs.

Teaching and learning strategies for early childhood are on pages 47-51.

Children (Grades 1-6)

Elementary-age children have slightly longer attention spans than younger children do. They are rapidly mastering the abilities of reading and writing; they can work together as a group; they are able to follow and remember the sequence of actions and characters in a story; and they are capable of cause-and-effect reasoning about the consequences of various courses of action. Still, they share many characteristics of younger children.

Children in grades 1-6 are capable of learning through listening, reading, observing, interacting, asking questions, experimenting, and any combination of approaches. However, as their verbal skills increase, they gradually become skillful at giving the "right" answers. Effective teaching helps nudge children to seriously consider the claims of Jesus Christ in their lives.

Teaching and learning strategies for children are on pages 52-56.

Youth (Grades 6-12)

Bizarre hair styles, outlandish clothes, annoying music, and unintelligible speech patterns tend to be common marks of the nearly adult of our species. When adults think about teenagers, they usually think of whatever it is that adolescents are currently doing to distinguish themselves from the rest of the human race.

Teaching anything, especially the Bible, to these hormone-driven humans is a major challenge. Much of the challenge involves responding appropriately to their urgent desire to be rid of all childish things, while resisting the responsibilities that come with adulthood. The teacher who gives even the slightest hint of "talking down" to them is immediately classified as out of touch, and the teacher who sounds too much like an adult is obviously a hopeless old fogey.

Thus, youth leaders and teachers feel an intense pressure to "relate," to know the latest about everything. In addition, many youth workers believe that anything that is being done with any other age level in the church could not possible work with youth. They constantly strive to come up with something new.

Unfortunately, in the push to be current and new, many people who attempt to teach teenagers overlook this fact: The basic human learning mechanisms that worked so efficiently when the child was two are still in place when the child hits twelve. The processes of receiving and organizing information, of retaining what was discovered, of evaluating reality, of applying truth to life situations, are more fully developed than in the younger years, but are still very similar. Therefore, successful teaching methods for teenagers stimulate the same learning skills that young people have been developing and expanding throughout their lives.

The middle school and high school years are times of learning more than facts. Teenagers are anxious to learn about meaning and significance. They want to know what lies beneath the surface. Effective teaching accepts their questions as well as their often frustrating inclination to doubt the answers they are given.

Teaching and learning strategies for youth are on pages 57-61.

Adult (Ages 18 and Up)

Jesus is almost universally acclaimed, even by those who deny his deity, as the Master

Teacher. He is granted this title both because of what he taught and how he taught it. Sadly, far too few of his followers, while seeking to teach the same truths, have emulated his example of using a wide variety of approaches to communicate God's truth to adults. Too many teachers of adults settle into a comfortable routine with very predictable presentations that often result in very predictable responses from class members.

Because teachers of adults do not have to contend with the wiggles and giggles of active, restless children and teenagers, they tend to assume that a group of mature, polite adults learn best by sitting passively and listening. While adults do tend to have better listening skills than children and youth, it is no indication that their minds and spirits no longer stretch. On the contrary, the Bible, written by adults, for adults, and almost totally about adults, provides a wealth of stimulating truth that should spark any group of adults out of their familiar routines.

At the same time a teacher of adults seeks to challenge and stimulate people, he/she must also maintain balance through a healthy respect for contemporary adult learners. Adults come with a lifetime of experience that prepares them to thoughtfully consider the practical implications of Bible content, even though they may have little or no Bible background.

Teaching and learning strategies for adults are on pages 63-66.

Learning Activities

People of all ages need to be actively involved in the learning process. The passing of years and the gaining of experiences does not fundamentally modify the manner in which human beings learn. Just because we become capable of sitting still for longer periods of time as we grow older does not mean that learning becomes a progressively more passive procedure. All of us need a varied combination of experiences—visual, auditory, physical, social, and emotional. This is especially true if our learning is intended to move us to changes in attitudes and behavior, and not just to accumulate more interesting tidbits of information to be stored away for use in a game of Bible trivia.

At the same time, specific methods are more appropriate for some age groups than others. Some individuals learn more efficiently through some approaches than do others in the same age range. Thus, effective teachers at all age levels seek to provide a balanced and varied diet of learning experiences.

Distribute the "Learning Activities" chart on pages 67-70 among your teachers to aid them in evaluating their current range of instructional procedures and to encourage them in expanding the methods used in their teaching.

1. Instruct teachers to choose several activities that are marked for the age group they teach, but that they have not used recently.

2. Invite teachers of similar age groups to share with each other the activities they marked.

3. Lead the teachers in discussing the possible uses of those approaches with the groups they teach. Ask:

How might this activity contribute to Bible learning? life application? relationship building?

In what type of lesson might this activity be most useful?

What preparation/explanation/procedures would be needed to make this activity a successful learning experience?

Teaching and Learning Strategies for Early Childhood

Mark the actions to rate your present and planned teaching efforts for young children. Space is provided in each section for additional ideas.

E=Excellent
S=Satisfactorily
   Doing Now
I=Improvement Needed
N=Need to Start

Set Meaningful Learning Objectives

___ 1. Our curriculum resources effectively aid teachers in planning and leading clearly focused sessions that help children understand biblical truth and apply it in daily living. The content of the sessions is appropriate for young children's comprehension levels.

___ 2. Session objectives are stated so that teachers can evaluate whether or not the children accomplish the desired learning. Thus, objectives describe what children will do or say to demonstrate what they have learned, rather than the objectives describing what teachers will do.

___ 3. All components (activities, music, Bible story, verse, etc.) of each session are planned to contribute to the accomplishment of the learning aim.

___ 4. _____

_____

Make Effective Use of Time

___ 1. Teachers involve children productively as soon as they arrive. For example, they provide a choice of two or more active learning experiences in which children may participate.

___ 2. Teachers follow a schedule that provides the security of familiar patterns while allowing flexibility and variety. The schedule enables young children to start with first-hand, active learning experiences that prepare them for the presentation of the Bible story. A sample schedule is on the next page.

___ 3. Teachers provide a balanced pattern of learning experiences: some quiet and some active, some familiar and some new, some done in large groups, some in small groups, and some done individually.

___ 4. All groups for young children follow a similar session plan, providing familiarity and stability for children, allowing teachers in different groups to benefit from sharing common experiences, and aiding leaders in efficiently training and guiding teachers.

A time schedule for young children must be very flexible. Teachers must be ready to cut short or extend an activity depending on the level of interest among the children. The suggested time periods in this chart assume a session of sixty to seventy-five minutes. As children grow older, they gradually become better able to learn in group settings.

Mark the actions to rate your present and planned teaching efforts for young children. Space is provided in each section for additional ideas.

> **E**=Excellent
> **S**=Satisfactorily
>   Doing Now
> **I**=Improvement Needed
> **N**=Need to Start

Babies/ Toddlers	Learning Activities offered continuously through the session	
2's & 3's	Learning Activities	45-50 minutes
	Group Singing/Worship/Bible Verse	10-15 minutes
	Bible Story/Activity	5-10 minutes
	TOTAL	60-75 minutes
	Transition to Next Hour	10-15 minutes
4's & 5's	Learning Activities	35-40 minutes
	Group Singing/Worship/Bible Verse	10-15 minutes
	Bible Story/Activity	15-20 minutes
	TOTAL	60-75 minutes
	Transition to Next Hour	15 minutes
Kindergarten	Learning Activities	30-35 minutes
	Group Singing/Worship/Bible Verse	15-20 minutes
	Bible Story/Activity	15-20 minutes
	TOTAL	60-75 minutes
	Transition to Next Hour	15 minutes

___ 5. _____

_____

Provide Positive Guidance

___ 1. Leaders and teachers of young children are carefully chosen through a clearly defined system of screening in which the safety of each child is the first priority.

___ **Background Check:** Leaders must request background information and check references on anyone who is allowed to work with young children. Questions must be asked and satisfactorily answered about a person's fitness to be with children. (*An information form is included in Chapter 7.*)

___ **Personal Knowledge:** Leaders must personally know anyone who would work with children. Leaders may personally know an individual prior to his/her time of service with children, or they may spend time getting to know the individual and observing him/her with children.

___ **Instruction:** The church must provide training for all who interact with children both in effective teaching procedures and in appropriate means of guiding behavior, which includes defining limits on verbal and physical contacts with children.

___ _____

_____

Mark the actions to rate your present and planned teaching efforts for young children. Space is provided in each section for additional ideas.

E=Excellent
S=Satisfactorily
    Doing Now
I=Improvement Needed
N=Need to Start

___ 2. Leaders and teachers demonstrate qualities of positive Christian living so that they may serve as examples to children of the values the church promotes.

    ___ **Church Attendance:** Consistent participation in the life of the congregation is important both for its contribution to the life of the individual as well as for the opportunities it affords for additional positive contacts with children and parents.

    ___ **Personal Devotion:** Evidence of a regular pattern of personal prayer and Bible study is a positive indicator of a person who desires to grow.

    ___ **Family Stability:** Persons who work with children should have a daily living environment that provides emotional and spiritual support. Persons who are undergoing stress at home and/or at work may find working with children is a positive outlet, but they should be provided with ongoing encouragement and assistance.

    ___ **Integrity:** The personal and business life of anyone who works with children must be marked by honesty and openness. Young children do not need perfect people as their teachers and leaders, but they do need people who will admit their mistakes and learn from them.

    ___ **Acceptance of Guidance:** A person who expects children to follow his/her leadership must be willing to follow the leadership of those the church has appointed as supervisors.

    ___ _____

    _____

___ 3. Leaders and teachers are chosen to reflect the diversity of people involved in the life of the church. Young children benefit greatly from interaction with men and women, older and younger adults, teens, couples and singles, and people from varied ethnic backgrounds.

___ 4. For the protection of both children and workers, at least two responsible persons should be present with any group at all times. Supervisors should regularly be present for observation and support.

___ 5. _____

_____

**Teaching and Learning
Strategies for
Early Childhood
3**

Plan Valid Learning Procedures

___ 1. Appropriate learning activities for young children lend themselves to easy connections to the Bible learning and life application emphasis of the session.

___ **Art:** Young children need opportunities for creative art experiences more than they need patterned craft projects. Art activities should help children relax and share their thoughts and feelings and not put them under pressure to "do it right."

___ **Blocks/Puzzles/Manipulative Toys:** Young children need many different kinds of objects to touch and use. The attraction of using interesting materials is often the teacher's best means of connecting Bible truth to the child's firsthand experiences.

___ **Created Wonders:** No child can resist the opportunity to explore living things (i.e., plants and occasionally a few animals) and other objects from God's fascinating world of creation.

___ **Family Living/Cooking:** A few simple props and the fertile imaginations of young children can turn any corner of an early childhood classroom into the scene of dramatic play as children live out familiar situations in which God's Word can be applied. Few activities capture interest and involve children in cooperative learning more than preparing food.

___ **Books/Pictures:** Positive conversation occurs as children and a teacher look together at books and pictures illustrating lesson related situations.

___ **Music/Rhythm:** A wide variety of music and rhythm activities are valuable for building positive feelings, enabling children to participate with others, and aiding in learning and remembering key ideas and Bible verses.

___ **Bible Stories/Verses:** A child's attitude and understanding are significantly influenced through learning stories and verses dealing with situations similar to those the child has faced.

___ **Video/Puppets/Media:** While young children are attracted to presentations on a TV screen, puppet stage, or some other form of media, teachers must be careful to present to children content and examples that support learning goals. (*See #3 below for guidelines on presenting content to young children.*)

___ _____

___ _____

Mark the actions to rate your present and planned teaching efforts for young children. Space is provided in each section for additional ideas.

E=Excellent
S=Satisfactorily
    Doing Now
I=Improvement Needed
N=Need to Start

___ 2. Teachers engage children in conversation about the session's learning objective before, during, and after they participate in an activity.

___ **Explanations:** Teachers consistently state the point of an activity. When introducing children to a learning activity, a teacher might say, "In our family center, we're pretending to get ready for bed so that we can learn about some of the ways God cares for us."

___ **Questions:** Teachers frequently ask questions planned to stimulate thought, not just about the activity, but about the intended Bible learning. For example, "You've painted a lot of stars in your sky picture. How big a paper would you need to paint as many stars as God

**Teaching and Learning
Strategies for
Early Childhood
4**

Mark the actions to rate your present and planned teaching efforts for young children. Space is provided in each section for additional ideas.

E=Excellent
S=Satisfactorily
　　Doing Now
I=Improvement Needed
N=Need to Start

put in the real sky?" Or, "What was something you thought about helping others while you were putting that puzzle together?"

___ **Songs:** Teachers regularly sing lesson-related songs while children are engaged in activities, linking what the child is doing to specific lesson content. For example, as children build with blocks, the teacher sings new words to the tune of "Here We Go 'Round the Mulberry Bush." "This is the way we take turns and share, . . . 'cause sharing shows us God's love."

___ **Bible Verse/Story:** Teachers look for ways to link the children's activity to the Bible verse or story. For example, "You were very kind to share the magnifying glass with Felipe. Your kindness reminded me of a Bible verse. Did you know the Bible says, 'Be kind to one another'?"

___ _____

_____

___ 3. Teachers express content in ways appropriate to the natural thought patterns of young children, limiting or avoiding vocabulary and ideas that they might misunderstand.

　　___ a. Because young children think literally, limit the use of symbolic language. Emphasize concepts that can be communicated simply and concretely.

　　___ b. Link new ideas to familiar experiences of the child and/or to first-hand learning experiences provided in the group.

　　___ c. Focus on one major concept at a time, not confusing children by presenting a variety of ideas.

　　___ d. Seek to engage the child physically and verbally, allowing the child to provide feedback for ideas that have been presented. Limit one-way presentations, and when used, offer time for children to put into practice and to talk about what they have seen and heard.

　　___ e. _____

_____

___ 4. Teachers provide adequate space and equipment to encourage young children in active learning. (*See Chapter 8.*)

___ 5. _____

_____

Teaching and Learning Strategies for Early Childhood
5

Teaching and Learning Strategies for Children

Mark the actions to rate your present and planned teaching efforts for elementary children. Space is provided in each section for additional ideas.

E=Excellent
S=Satisfactorily
   Doing Now
I=Improvement Needed
N=Need to Start

Set Meaningful Learning Objectives

___ 1. Our curriculum resources effectively aid teachers in planning and leading clearly focused sessions that help children understand biblical truth and apply it in daily living. The content of the sessions is appropriate for elementary children's comprehension levels.

___ 2. Session objectives are stated so that teachers can evaluate whether or not the children accomplish the desired learning. Thus, objectives describe what children will do or say to demonstrate what they have learned, rather than the objectives describing what teachers will do.

___ 3. All components (activities, music, Bible story, verse, etc.) of each session are planned to contribute to the accomplishment of the learning aim.

___ 4. _____

_____

Make Effective Use of Time

___ 1. Teachers involve children productively as soon as they arrive. For example, provide a choice of two or more active learning experiences in which children may participate.

___ 2. Teachers follow a schedule that provides the security of familiar patterns while allowing flexibility and variety. The sequence of learning experiences builds from areas of children's interest to exploring, understanding, and applying Bible truth. A sample schedule follows:

The suggested time periods in this chart assume a session of sixty to seventy-five minutes in length.

Welcome and Introduce Topic	10-15 minutes plus presession
Bible Story and Review	15-20 minutes
Application Activities, Worship, and Relationship Building	35-40 minutes
TOTAL	60-75 minutes
Transition to Next Hour	15 minutes

3. Teachers provide a balanced pattern of learning experiences: some quiet and some active, some familiar and some new, some done in large groups, some in small groups, and some done individually.

4. All groups for elementary-age children follow a similar session plan, providing familiarity for children, allowing teachers in different groups to benefit from sharing common experiences, and aiding leaders in efficiently training and guiding teachers.

5. _____

_____

Mark the actions to rate your present and planned teaching efforts for elementary children. Space is provided in each section for additional ideas.

E=Excellent
S=Satisfactorily
 Doing Now
I=Improvement Needed
N=Need to Start

Provide Positive Guidance

1. Leaders and teachers of children are carefully chosen through a clearly defined system of screening in which the safety of each child is the first priority.

 Background Check: Leaders must request background information and check references on anyone who is allowed to work with children. Questions must be asked and satisfactorily answered about a person's fitness to be with children. (*An information form is included in Chapter 7.*)

 Personal Knowledge: Leaders must personally know anyone who would work with children. Leaders may personally know an individual prior to his/her service with children, or they may spend time getting to know the individual and observing him/her with children.

 Instruction: The church must provide training for all who interact with children both in effective teaching procedures and in appropriate means of guiding behavior, which includes defining limits on verbal and physical contacts with children.

_____

_____

2. Leaders and teachers demonstrate qualities of positive Christian living so that they may serve as examples to children of the values the church promotes.

 Church Attendance: Consistent participation in the life of the congregation is important both for its contribution to the life of the individual as well as for the opportunities it affords for additional positive contacts with children and parents.

 Personal Devotion: Evidence of a regular pattern of personal prayer and Bible study is a positive indicator of a person who desires to grow.

 Family Stability: Persons who work with children should have a daily living environment that provides emotional and spiritual support. Persons who are undergoing stress at home and/or at work may find

working with children is a positive outlet, but they should be provided with ongoing encouragement and assistance.

___ **Integrity:** The personal and business life of anyone who works with children must be marked by honesty and openness. Children do not need perfect people as their teachers and leaders, but they do need people who will admit their mistakes and learn from them.

___ **Acceptance of Guidance:** A person who expects children to follow his/her leadership must be willing to follow the leadership of those the church has appointed as supervisors.

___ _____

_____

___ 3. Leaders and teachers should be chosen to reflect the diversity of people involved in the life of the church. Children benefit greatly from interaction with both men and women, older and younger adults, teens, couples and singles, and people from varied ethnic backgrounds.

___ 4. For the protection of both children and workers, at least two responsible persons should be present with any group at all times. Supervisors should regularly be present for observation and support.

___ 5. _____

_____

Plan Valid Learning Procedures

___ 1. Appropriate learning activities for children lend themselves to easy connections to the Bible learning and life application emphasis of the session.

___ **Art:** Children need opportunities for creative art experiences that allow them to express thoughts and feelings about what they are learning. Children's art often reveals insights and understanding (or misunderstandings) that verbal interaction alone would miss. Because children's judgment of art often surpasses their ability to produce it, care must be taken not to stress artistic skill.

___ **Games/Puzzles:** Games are usually welcomed with enthusiasm and are valuable means of reviewing content, practicing Bible verses, encouraging relationships, and stimulating thought about issues reflected in the game. The use of games must be tempered with awareness that competition in games sometimes undermines the positive values being taught. Keep the emphasis on cooperation, not winning and losing.

___ **Research:** As children's reading skills advance, they become increasingly capable of using a variety of resources to discover information.

Mark the actions to rate your present and planned teaching efforts for elementary children. Space is provided in each section for additional ideas.

E=Excellent
S=Satisfactorily Doing Now
I=Improvement Needed
N=Need to Start

Teaching and Learning Strategies for Children
3

A Bible dictionary, atlas, and concordance are very useful learning tools, so are teaching pictures, cassette tapes, charts, and interviews with knowledgeable people.

___ **Service Projects:** Children thrive when given meaningful opportunities to do good for others. Whether fixing a snack for another age group, preparing a mural to display for the rest of the congregation, picking up trash, or making puzzles, children enjoy discovering how blessed it is to give.

___ **Drama:** Children enjoy participating in simple skits, role plays, pantomimes, script reading, and other drama activities. While drama activities may elicit some silliness, they can also be effective means of presenting or reviewing Bible story information or of stimulating thought about how Bible truth applies to life situations.

___ **Music/Rhythm:** A wide variety of music and rhythm activities is valuable for building positive feelings, helping children to participate with others, and aiding in learning and remembering key ideas and Bible verses. Grade schoolers are as influenced by music today as teenagers were a generation ago.

___ **Bible Stories/Verses:** A child's attitude and understanding is significantly influenced through learning stories and verses dealing with situations similar to those the child has faced.

___ **Video/Puppets/Media:** While children are attracted to presentations on a TV screen, puppet stage, or some other form of media, teachers must be careful to present to children concepts and examples that support learning goals. (*See #3 below for guidelines on presenting content to children.*)

___ **Relationship Building:** While alert teachers should use all learning activities to build their own relationships with children and children's relationships with one another, some activities may be provided that focus specifically on encouraging friendships to grow. Snacks, recognition of birthdays and visitors, and giving of awards can all be used to help children enjoy getting to know one another better. At the same time, teachers must be cautious about embarrassing a child who does not want group recognition.

___ _____

___ _____

___ 2. Teachers engage children in conversation about the session's learning objective before, during, and after they participate in an activity.

___ **Explanations:** Teachers consistently state the point of an activity. When introducing children to a learning activity, a teacher might say, "We're putting the words of this Bible verse together to help us learn two important things God wants us to do."

___ **Questions:** Teachers frequently ask questions planned to stimulate thought, not just about the activity, but about the intended Bible

---

Mark the actions to rate your present and planned teaching efforts for elementary children. Space is provided in each section for additional ideas.

    E=Excellent
    S=Satisfactorily
        Doing Now
   I=Improvement Needed
  N=Need to Start

Teaching and Learning Strategies for Children
4

Mark the actions to rate your present and planned teaching efforts for elementary children. Space is provided in each section for additional ideas.

E=Excellent
S=Satisfactorily
    Doing Now
I=Improvement Needed
N=Need to Start

learning. For example, "If you had been a friend of King Saul's, what advice would you have given him?" Or, "Why do you think trusting in the Lord is better than leaning on our own understanding?"

___ **Songs:** Teachers regularly use lesson-related songs to reinforce key ideas the child should remember. Songs are selected because of their value in supporting the lesson focus.

___ **Bible Verse/Story:** Teachers look for ways to link the children's activity to the Bible verse or story. For example, "Some of you wrote down some good examples of times when it is hard to do right. Our story today is about a woman who had a very hard thing to do. Let's find out what made the difference for her in either doing or not doing the right thing."

___ _____

_____

___ 3. Teachers express content in ways appropriate to the natural thought patterns of children, limiting or avoiding vocabulary and ideas that they might misunderstand.

    ___ a. Because children think literally, they need careful explanations of symbolic language. Whenever possible, use concepts that can be communicated simply and concretely.

    ___ b. Link new ideas to familiar experiences of the child. Show how the truth being studied connects to the child's own life and to the experiences of others known to the child.

    ___ c. Focus on one major concept at a time, not confusing children by presenting a variety of ideas.

    ___ d. Seek to engage each child physically and verbally, allowing the child to provide feedback for ideas that have been presented. Limit one-way presentations, and when used, offer time for children to practice and talk about what they have seen and heard.

    ___ e. _____

_____

___ 4. Teachers provide adequate space and equipment to encourage children in active learning. (_See Chapter 8._)

___ 5. _____

_____

Teaching and Learning Strategies for Children
5

Teaching and Learning Strategies for Youth

Mark the actions to rate your present and planned teaching efforts for middle and high school youth. Space is provided in each section for additional ideas.

E=Excellent
S=Satisfactorily Doing Now
I=Improvement Needed
N=Need to Start

Set Meaningful Learning Objectives

___ 1. Our curriculum resources effectively aid teachers in planning and leading clearly focused sessions that help teens understand biblical truth and apply it in daily living.

___ 2. Session objectives are stated so that teachers and leaders can evaluate whether or not young people accomplish the desired learning. Thus, objectives describe what learners will do or say to demonstrate what they have learned, rather than the objectives describing what teachers will do.

___ 3. All components (activities, music, Bible study, etc.) of each session are planned to contribute to the accomplishment of the learning aim.

___ 4. _____

_____

Make Effective Use of Time

___ 1. Teachers involve teens productively as soon as they arrive. For example, they provide a choice of two or more small group learning and sharing experiences in which teens and teachers participate.

___ 2. Teachers follow a flexible schedule that balances familiar patterns with flexibility and variety. The sequence of activities starts with items of interest to teens, then guides them in studying, analyzing and applying Bible truth. A sample schedule follows:

The suggested time periods in this chart assume a session of sixty to seventy-five minutes in length.

Teaching and Learning Strategies for Youth
1

Welcome and Introduce Topic	10-15 minutes plus presession
Bible Study	25-30 minutes
Application Activity	20 minutes
Decision Activity	5-10 minutes
TOTAL	60-75 minutes

___ 3. Teachers provide a balanced pattern of learning experiences: some quiet and some active, some familiar and some new, some done in large groups, some in small groups, and some done individually.

___ 4. All groups for teens follow similar patterns of flexible session plans, providing both familiarity and variety for learners, allowing teachers in different groups to benefit from sharing common experiences, and aiding leaders in efficiently training and guiding teachers.

___ 5. _____

_____

Mark the actions to rate your present and planned teaching efforts for middle and high school youth. Space is provided in each section for additional ideas.

E=Excellent
S=Satisfactorily Doing Now
I=Improvement Needed
N=Need to Start

Provide Positive Guidance

___ 1. Leaders and teachers of youth are carefully chosen through a clearly defined system of screening in which the spiritual, emotional, and physical well-being of each young person is the first priority.

___ **Background Check:** Leaders must request background information and check references on anyone who is allowed to work with teens. Questions must be asked and satisfactorily answered about a person's fitness to be with adolescents. (*An information form is included in Chapter 7.*)

___ **Personal Knowledge:** Leaders must personally know anyone who would work with teenagers. Leaders may personally know an individual prior to his/her service with teenagers, or they may spend time getting to know the individual and observing him/her with teenagers.

___ **Instruction:** The church must provide training for all who interact with youth both in effective teaching procedures and in appropriate means of guiding behavior, which includes defining limits on verbal and physical contacts with teens.

___ _____

_____

___ 2. Leaders and teachers demonstrate qualities of positive Christian living so that they may serve as examples to young people of the values the church promotes.

___ **Church Attendance:** Consistent participation in the life of the congregation is important both for its contribution to the life of the individual as well as for the opportunities it affords for additional positive contacts with teens and their parents.

___ **Personal Devotion:** Evidence of a regular pattern of personal prayer and Bible study is a positive indicator of a person who desires to grow.

Teaching and Learning Strategies for Youth

2

Mark the actions to rate your present and planned teaching efforts for middle and high school youth. Space is provided in each section for additional ideas.

E=Excellent
S=Satisfactorily
   Doing Now
I=Improvement Needed
N=Need to Start

___ **Family Stability:** Persons who work with teens should have a daily living environment that provides emotional and spiritual support. Persons who are undergoing stress at home and/or at work may find working with young people is a positive outlet, but they should be provided with ongoing encouragement and assistance.

___ **Integrity:** The personal and business life of anyone who works with teens must be marked by honesty and openness. Teenagers do not need perfect people as their teachers and leaders, but they do need people who will admit their mistakes and demonstrate a willingness to learn from them.

___ **Acceptance of Guidance:** A person who expects teens to follow his/her leadership must be willing to follow the leadership of those the church has appointed as supervisors.

___ _____

_____

___ 3. Leaders and teachers should be chosen to reflect the diversity of people involved in the life of the church. Teens benefit greatly from interaction with both men and women, older and younger adults, couples and singles, and people from varied ethnic backgrounds.

___ 4. For the protection of both teenagers and workers, at least two responsible persons should be present with any group at all times. Supervisors should regularly be present for observation and support. It is wise to require that one-to-one ministry to teens be done by persons of the same sex and at a time and place when other responsible persons are available for support.

___ 5. _____

_____

Plan Valid Learning Procedures

___ 1. Learning activities are chosen for teens that enable teachers to make easy connections to the Bible learning and life application emphasis of the session.

___ **Bible Study:** Teenagers are able to explore a wide variety of biblical material in addition to stories. They respond well to passages from the epistles, Psalms, and Proverbs, as well as to some of the sermons of Jesus, Paul and Old Testament prophets. Teens tend to be most interested in finding out what the Bible says when they discover that it deals with issues of concern to them. Teachers involve students in using the Bible themselves, discovering what God's Word says about the issues being discussed.

Mark the actions to rate your present and planned teaching efforts for middle and high school youth. Space is provided in each section for additional ideas.

E=Excellent
S=Satisfactorily
   Doing Now
I=Improvement Needed
N=Need to Start

Teaching and Learning Strategies for Youth

4

____ **Lecture:** A verbal presentation of information is often the most efficient way to present a body of information to a group. A skillful speaker can entertain, inform, and motivate listeners. With young people, lecture is usually most effective when interspersed with a variety of involving activities, introducing, explaining, or summarizing important points. The main drawbacks to a lecture are that learners' minds may easily be engaged elsewhere and that hearing is only one part of the learning process. Unless learners are led to follow their hearing with other responses, little or no lasting change in understanding, attitude, or action is likely to take place.

____ **Discussion/Question and Answer:** Teachers ask questions to promote participation and stimulate thought about Bible content, its meaning, and its application. Teachers phrase questions to encourage open sharing of ideas, not just to seek answers. Young people love to hear themselves talk, and they have ideas on many topics. Engaging them in verbal interaction is a valuable way to keep them mentally involved, to help them grow in understanding of each other, and to guide them toward a fuller understanding of the lesson topic. Be aware that in any group of teens, especially when boys and girls are together, there is a very strong tendency for young people to give responses that they think will impress others, rather than to expand their learning.

____ **Video/Media:** Teenagers view television as a means of entertainment, not as an aid to learning. Thoughtful selection of video or other media (audio tape, slides, computer) can be a helpful way to secure attention or stimulate thoughtful discussion. Often, brief clips followed by guided interaction are more effective in instructional settings than more lengthy presentations.

____ **Art:** Young people enjoy opportunities for carefully selected art activities that allow them to express thoughts and feelings about their experiences and what they are learning. Art activities are often useful ways to involve teenagers in cooperative group interaction. Usually, art activities work best when a light-hearted approach is needed for stimulating thought about a topic.

____ **Games:** Games may occasionally be used for a change of pace in reviewing content and encouraging relationships. Be cautious of using games that require Bible knowledge, since students who lack that background may feel excluded.

____ **Research:** Young people are capable of using a variety of tools to discover information: Bible dictionary, atlas, concordance, and so on. Students are also challenged by comparing Bible passages to discover points of emphasis, differences, or commonalities.

____ **Service Projects:** Young people are eager to work together on projects that benefit others, and they have the energy and skills to do a variety of useful work. Teachers and leaders who schedule opportunities for service projects also find them to be ideal means of building interest and enthusiasm.

Mark the actions to rate your present and planned teaching efforts for middle and high school youth. Space is provided in each section for additional ideas.

E=Excellent
S=Satisfactorily
　　Doing Now
I=Improvement Needed
N=Need to Start

___ **Music:** Some youth groups avoid music as though it were a plague. Others find it a powerfully unifying and motivating tool. Besides group singing, which requires a leader with skill, enthusiasm, and rapport with group members, teens enjoy and learn from listening to music, both live and recorded (including audio and video). Music with a contemporary sound and a clear message that is related to the session topic can attract attention, stimulate a discussion, or provide a means of response to what has been learned.

___ _____

_____

___ 2. Teachers provide adequate space and a comfortable environment that invites young people to participate as part of group experiences. (*See Chapter 8.*)

___ 3. _____

_____

Teaching and Learning Strategies for Adults

Mark the actions to rate your present and planned teaching efforts for adults. Space is provided in each section for additional ideas.

E=Excellent
S=Satisfactorily
　Doing Now
I=Improvement Needed
N=Need to Start

The suggested time periods in this chart assume a session of sixty to seventy-five minutes in length.

Teaching and Learning Strategies for Adults

1

Set Meaningful Learning Objectives

___ 1. Our curriculum resources effectively aid teachers in planning and leading clearly focused sessions that help adults understand biblical truth and apply it in daily living.

___ 2. Session objectives are stated so that teachers can evaluate whether or not adults accomplish the desired learning. Thus, objectives describe what adults will do or say to demonstrate what they have learned, rather than describing what teachers will do.

___ 3. All components (activities, music, Bible study, etc.) of each session are planned to contribute to the accomplishment of the learning aim.

___ 4. _____

_____

Make Effective Use of Time

___ 1. Teachers involve adults productively as soon as they arrive. For example, they provide a stimulating quotation or question to engage group members in conversation related to the session topic.

___ 2. Teachers follow a flexible schedule that balances familiar patterns with flexibility and variety. The sequence of activities starts with items of interest to adults, then guides them in studying, analyzing and applying Bible truth. A sample schedule follows:

Fellowship and Introduce Topic	10-15 minutes plus presession
Bible Study	30-40 minutes
Application and Decision Activities	20 minutes
TOTAL	60-75 minutes

___ 3. Teachers provide a balanced pattern of learning experiences: some familiar and some new, some done in large groups, some in small groups, and some done individually.

Mark the actions to rate your present and planned teaching efforts for adults. Space is provided in each section for additional ideas.

E=Excellent
S=Satisfactorily Doing Now
I=Improvement Needed
N=Need to Start

___ 4. All groups for adults follow similar patterns of flexible session plans, providing both familiarity and variety for learners, allowing teachers in different groups to benefit from sharing common experiences, and aiding leaders in efficiently training and guiding teachers.

___ 5. _____

_____

Provide Positive Guidance

___ 1. Leaders and teachers of adults are carefully chosen through a clearly defined system of screening in which the personal and spiritual growth of adult participants is the first priority.

   ___ **Background Check:** Leaders must request background information and check references on anyone who is enlisted to teach adults. Questions must be asked and satisfactorily answered about a person's fitness to lead. (*An information form is included in Chapter 7.*)

   ___ **Personal Knowledge:** Leaders must personally know anyone who would teach adults. Leaders may personally know an individual prior to his/her service with adults, or they may spend time getting to know the individual and observing him/her interacting with adults.

   ___ **Instruction:** The church must provide training for all who would teach adults both in effective teaching procedures and in appropriate means of building healthy relationships.

   ___ _____

   _____

___ 2. Teachers demonstrate qualities of positive Christian living so that they may serve as examples of the values the church promotes.

   ___ **Church Attendance:** Consistent participation in the life of the congregation is important both for its contribution to the life of the individual as well as for the opportunities it affords for additional positive contacts with group members.

   ___ **Personal Devotion:** Evidence of a regular pattern of personal prayer and Bible study is a positive indicator of a person who desires to grow.

   ___ **Family Stability:** Persons who teach adults should have a daily living environment that provides emotional and spiritual support. Persons who are undergoing stress at home and/or at work may find teaching is a positive outlet, but they should be provided with ongoing encouragement and assistance.

   ___ **Integrity:** The personal and business life of anyone who teaches adults must be marked by honesty and openness. Teachers do not need to be

perfect, but they do need to be people who will admit their mistakes and demonstrate a willingness to learn from them.

___ **Acceptance of Guidance:** A person who expects others to follow his/her leadership must be willing to follow the leadership of those the church has appointed as supervisors.

___ _____

_____

Mark the actions to rate your present and planned teaching efforts for adults. Space is provided in each section for additional ideas.

E=Excellent
S=Satisfactorily
    Doing Now
I=Improvement Needed
N=Need to Start

___ 3. Leaders and teachers should be chosen to reflect the diversity of people involved in the life of the church. All adults benefit greatly from interaction with both men and women, older and younger adults, couples and singles, and people with varied ethnic backgrounds.

___ 4. _____

_____

Plan Valid Learning Procedures

___ 1. Learning activities are chosen that enable teachers to clearly present Bible truth and connect it to the lives of adults in the group.

___ **Bible Study:** Adults respond positively to opportunities to explore biblical content. They need the challenge of finding out for themselves what the Bible says and of wrestling with its implications for them today.

___ **Lecture:** A verbal presentation of information is often the most efficient way to present a body of information to a group. A skillful speaker can entertain, inform, and motivate listeners. While most adults are able to listen to a speaker, lecture is usually most effective when interspersed with other involving activities, introducing, explaining, or summarizing important points. The main drawbacks to a lecture are that learners' minds may easily be engaged elsewhere and that hearing is only one part of the learning process. Unless learners are led to follow their hearing with other responses, little or no lasting change in understanding, attitude, or action is likely to take place.

___ **Discussion/Question and Answer:** Teachers ask questions to promote participation and stimulate thought about Bible content, its meaning, and its application. Teachers phrase questions to encourage open sharing of ideas, not just to seek answers. Adults have ideas on many topics. Engaging adults in verbal interaction is a valuable way to keep them mentally involved, to help them grow in understanding of each other, and to guide them toward a fuller understanding of the lesson topic. There is always a danger that people may assume that having talked about a truth, they have learned it. Teachers must consistently prod participants to move beyond talking about the Christian life to actually living it.

Mark the actions to rate your present and planned teaching efforts for adults. Space is provided in each section for additional ideas.

E=Excellent
S=Satisfactorily
　　Doing Now
I=Improvement Needed
N=Need to Start

___ **Video/Media:** Television has great appeal, but it also lulls people into a spectator mode in which they are able to distance themselves from what they see and hear. Thoughtful selection of video or other media (audio tape, slides, computer) can be a helpful way to secure attention or stimulate thoughtful discussion. Often, brief clips followed by guided interaction are more effective in instructional settings than are more lengthy presentations.

___ **Art:** Occasionally adults enjoy simple art activities that allow them to express thoughts and feelings about their experiences and what they are learning. Art activities are often nonthreatening ways to involve adults in cooperative group interaction. Usually, art activities work best when a light-hearted approach is needed for stimulating thought about a topic.

___ **Games:** Games may occasionally be used for a change of pace in reviewing content and encouraging relationships. Be cautious about using games that require previous Bible knowledge, since adults who lack that background may feel excluded.

___ **Service Projects:** Some of the best learning teachers can provide adult groups is to lead them to work together in projects that benefit others. Teachers and leaders who schedule opportunities for service projects also find them ideal means of building interest and enthusiasm.

___ **Music:** Adult groups that use music have traditionally used it for a variety of purposes: worship, group participation, keeping something going until all the late-comers are in place, and so on. The powerful benefit of music as an aid to learning is often not considered in the selection of music. This pattern is unfortunate. Music that expresses key thoughts from a session is a powerful means of aiding people in remembering those ideas and motivating them to act accordingly.

___ _____

_____

___ 2. Teachers provide adequate space and a comfortable environment that invites adults to participate as part of group experiences. (*See Chapter 8.*)

___ 3. _____

_____

Learning Activities

How might this activity contribute to
    Bible learning?
    life application?
    relationship building?

In what type of lesson might this activity be most useful?

What preparation/ explanation/procedures would be needed to make this activity a successful learning experience?

Learning Activities	Ages 2-6	Grades 1-2	Grades 3-6	Grades 6-12	Adults
ART					
Advertisement (magazine/newspaper)		•	•	•	•
Badges	•	•	•		
Banners		•	•	•	•
Billboard			•	•	•
Block/Gadget Printing	•	•			
Bulletin Board	•	•	•	•	•
Bumper Sticker			•	•	•
Cartooning	•	•	•	•	
Chalk Drawing	•	•	•		
Chart/Graph			•	•	•
Clay	•	•	•		•
Collage (gluing objects, paper, pictures, etc.)	•	•	•		•
Crayon Drawing	•	•			
Crayon Etchings (scratch design in crayon)		•	•		
Crayon Melting		•	•		
Crayon Rubbing	•	•	•		
Crayon/Paint Resist	•	•	•		
Diorama (scene)		•	•		
Doodles			•	•	•
Dough (salt/flour)	•	•			
Felt Marker Drawing		•	•	•	•
Frieze (series of scenes)		•	•	•	•
Mobiles		•	•		•
Montage (collage of words/pictures)		•	•		•
Mosaic (tile/paper)			•	•	•
Mural			•	•	•
Painting, Blow (straw)	•	•	•		
Painting, Brush/Tempera	•	•	•		
Painting, Finger	•	•	•		
Painting, Sand		•	•		
Painting, Sawdust			•		

How might this activity contribute to
Bible learning?
life application?
relationship building?

In what type of lesson might this activity be most useful?

What preparation/ explanation/procedures would be needed to make this activity a successful learning experience?

Learning Activities	Ages 2-6	Grades 1-2	Grades 3-6	Grades 6-12	Adults
Painting, String	•	•	•		
Painting, Water colors		•	•	•	
Paper Cutting		•	•		•
Paper Sculpture			•	•	
Paper Tearing	•	•	•	•	•
Papier-maché			•	•	
Posters		•	•	•	•
Rebus (pictures replace words/sounds)			•	•	
Silhouettes			•	•	•
Slides (writing/drawing)			•	•	•
Stained Glass (paper/ cellophane)			•	•	•
Tissue and Starch	•	•			
Transparencies		•	•	•	•
TV Box		•	•		
DRAMA					
Audio Recording	•	•	•		•
Block Building/Toys	•				
Dramatic Reading				•	•
Family Living (dolls)	•				
Monolog			•		•
Pantomime		•	•	•	•
Puppets	•	•	•	•	•
Radio Drama (play reading)			•	•	•
Role Play/Situations		•	•	•	•
Story, Act-it-Out	•	•	•	•	•
Tableau (picture posing/ photography)		•	•	•	•
Talk Show			•	•	•
Video Recording	•	•	•	•	•
DISCUSSION/QUESTION AND ANSWER					
Agree/Disagree Statements			•	•	•
Brainstorming			•	•	•
Case Study				•	•
Circle Response		•	•		•
Debate				•	•

How might this activity contribute to
    Bible learning?
    life application?
    relationship building?

In what type of lesson might this activity be most useful?

What preparation/explanation/procedures would be needed to make this activity a successful learning experience?

Learning Activities	Ages 2-6	Grades 1-2	Grades 3-6	Grades 6-12	Adults
Dialog		•	•	•	•
Idea Sharing	•	•	•	•	•
Interview/Survey		•	•	•	•
Listening Teams			•	•	•
Picture Response	•	•	•	•	•
Question/Answer	•	•	•	•	•
Small Group Interaction		•	•	•	•
Timed Response		•	•	•	•
Word Association					•
MUSIC/RHYTHM					
Choral Reading			•	•	•
Echo Song	•	•	•		
Fit Bible Verse to Music			•	•	•
Hymn Study				•	•
Instruments	•	•	•		
Listening	•	•	•		
Litany			•	•	•
Match Song with Bible Verse/Passage			•	•	•
Poetry Reading		•	•	•	•
Rap			•	•	
Rhythm Pattern for Verse		•	•		
Sign Language for Song	•	•	•		•
Singing	•	•	•	•	•
Write/Say New Words	•	•	•	•	•
RESEARCH					
Bible Atlas/Maps			•	•	•
Bible Dictionary		•	•	•	•
Bible Locating/Reading		•	•	•	•
Bible Study (inductive)			•	•	•
Books	•	•	•	•	•
Computer		•		•	•
Field Trip	•	•	•	•	•
Films	•	•	•	•	•
Filmstrips/Slides	•	•	•	•	•
Listening Center (audio cassette/record)	•	•	•	•	•

How might this activity
contribute to
　　Bible learning?
　　life application?
　　relationship building?

In what type of lesson might
this activity be most useful?

What preparation/
explanation/procedures
would be needed to make
this activity a successful
learning experience?

　　　T=Teacher
　　　L=Learner

Learning Activities	Ages 2-6	Grades 1-2	Grades 3-6	Grades 6-12	Adults
Overhead Transparency		•	•	•	•
Pictures/Photographs	•	•	•	•	•
Service Project	•	•	•	•	•
Survey/Census			•	•	•
Video	•	•	•	•	•
VERBAL COMMUNICATION *(also see Discussion)*					
Bible Reading (oral)	T	T/L	T/L	T/L	T/L
Chalk Talk			T	T/L	T/L
Conversation	T/L	T/L	T/L	T/L	T/L
Demonstration	T	T	T/L	T/L	T/L
Illustrated Lecture	T	T	T	T/L	T/L
Memory/Recitation	T/L	T/L	T/L	T/L	T/L
Object Lesson			T	T	T
One-Minute Message			L	L	L
Oral Report			L	L	L
Panel Presentation			T/L	T/L	T/L
Sermon			T	T/L	T/L
Storytelling	T	T/L	T/L	T/L	T/L
WRITING					
Acrostic			T/L	T/L	T/L
Bumper Sticker			L	L	L
Captions (for pictures)	T	T/L	T/L	L	L
Commercial/Slogan		L	L	L	L
Condensed Version				L	L
Crossword Puzzle			L	L	L
Diary/Journal			L	L	L
Dictation (adult writes)	T	T			
Graffiti			L	L	L
Letter/Memo/Note		L	L	L	L
List/Ranking	T	T/L	T/L	T/L	T/L
News Report			L	L	L
Parable				L	L
Paraphrase			L	L	L
Script			L	L	L

4
Grouping for Effective Learning

Q. When Jesus fed 5,000 people from a child's sack lunch, why did he have the disciples organize the crowd into groups of fifty?

A. So the disciples could distribute the food in an orderly fashion and make sure no one was overlooked.

Q. Why should a church that wants to build and maintain an effective teaching ministry be concerned about how it organizes (groups) people?

A. So the teachers can distribute the Word in an orderly fashion and make sure no one is overlooked.

While that is a good answer, far more is involved in organizing (grouping) learners than simply trying to fit everyone into a slot. People today defy most attempts to cram them into categories. For example:

"Let's have a class for single adults and a class for married adults. Oh, maybe we'll need two married classes—one for younger married people and one for older married people."

"I'm single and I feel more comfortable with some of my married friends."

"We're older, but we just got married, and we think we fit better with the younger group."

"Well, I just graduated from high school, and I don't fit in with the single adults or the married ones. I don't belong with the high school group anymore. I think I'll check out the church down the street."

"I think we should promote our preschoolers on their birthdays. If the sign on the door says three-year-olds, we can't keep someone in there after turning four."

"My child is so much more advanced than the others in there. She needs the challenge of being with older children."

"If her kid gets to move up, then my kid's moving up, too."

71

"At least we can set a policy for school-aged children. Just put them with their school grade and let it go at that."

"My son was kept back and is old enough to be in seventh grade. Since that's where all his friends are, we think he should be able to be with them."

"We've been home schooling our daughter, and she's so much more advanced than other kids her age."

You get the picture. Human beings are not easily categorized. We arrive as rugged individualists with no sense of group identity. Modern society goes to great lengths to encourage the former and discourage the latter.

Grouping Elements

While there are problems, church can benefit from having a clearly defined plan for providing people with productive, enjoyable groups for learning, fellowship, and service. Consider these factors:

Group Size

When groups of any age get too large, the overall effectiveness of the group experience diminishes. This is very noticeable with children, since groups that are too large quickly turn chaotic. While teens and adults don't start running amok when their groups are too large, numerous negatives exist when their groups consistently exceed optimum size.

- Learning efficiency drops as group members become spectators instead of active learners.
- Accountability diminishes as leaders are unable to interact personally with learners about their understanding and application of what is being taught.

- Relationships either narrow or tend toward superficial levels. In a large group it is not possible to know everyone well, so most people focus on the few people they do know well, or "graze" genially among the many they know slightly, or withdraw from interaction all together.

Large groups can, at times, provide benefits mainly with youth and adult groups.

- Large groups generate a level of energy that is exciting and motivating.
- They offer an attractive variety of people to get to know (very appealing to older youth and single adults).
- They provide the safety of anonymity to people who are hesitant about getting involved.

When recognizing the benefits of small groups and the attraction of large groups, youth and adult ministries can seek a balance between both group experiences. (*Chapter 5 discusses alternative models for youth and adult ministries. Chapter 9 has more information about small group ministries.*)

With all other things being equal (which, of course, they never are), a learner is better served in a small group than in a group that is too large.

Teacher-to-Learner Ratio

The number of learners for every teacher (leader, counselor, aide, etc.) in a group has a significant impact on the total effectiveness of that group. Occasionally, a leader with exceptional abilities will succeed with a large group and no visible supporting cast. A church should be very cautious about building a structure that will demand exceptional leadership in order to succeed. The age-level sections that follow present guidelines for the number of leadership personnel needed for the number of learners being reached.

With all other things being equal (which they still are not), a learner is better served in a group that has enough leadership to provide personal attention than in a group that is understaffed.

Comfort and Crowding Factors

Numerous other factors contribute to a group's feeling comfortable, crowded, or disconnected.

A room is too small for the number of people when it is difficult for people to interact with one another and to participate as active learners.

A room is too large for the number of people when people are scattered or surrounded by unused space.

Crowding can be enjoyable and exciting for brief periods, but the time comes when people become uncomfortable.

Furnishings and their arrangement have a significant impact on how long people can remain positive about a crowded situation.

With all other things being equal (and they are not equal yet), a learner is better served in a group where the setting is comfortable than in a group where the setting is uncomfortable.

Commonalities

People tend to feel most comfortable in groups of people who share similar life experiences and interests. The most obvious common factors are age, gender, and race.

- The only freshman in a high school group dominated by seniors will tend to feel out of place.

- A fourth grade girl looking into a room filled with fourth grade boys will think twice—maybe three or four times—about going inside.
- A person is likely to feel conspicuous in a group where everyone else is from a different racial background.

While Scripture clearly teaches that all these human differences are not to be barriers that separate Christians (Romans 10:12; 1 Corinthians 12:12; Galatians 3:28; Colossians 3:11), and while most of us have established deep kinships with others in spite of differences in age, gender, and race, we know that people tend to respond most readily to those with whom they easily identify.

With all other things being equal (dream on), a learner is better served in a group of similar age, interest, or other common factor than in a group where common bonds are lacking. (For example, our lone fourth grade girl might be better off in the fifth, or third, grade group with other girls, than in a class with all boys.)

Personal Needs and Flexibility

Thinking of our lone fourth grade girl, or that intimidated freshman boy, or any person in our churches and communities who does not fit easily into rigid structure, we discover that any church that seeks to build an effective teaching ministry must have a significant degree of organizational flexibility in order to meet personal needs. This is not a declaration to do away with a grouping plan, but to be willing, even eager, to adapt the plan to fit your people. Consider these problems.

Problem: It's time to promote children into the four-year-old group. If all those who fit the age range are moved, the group will be too large.

Solution: Narrow the age range this year for this group, either retaining some of the young fours in a three's and four's group or moving some older fours ahead into an older group. (It is usually more politically expedient to advance some children to the next group a little early rather than to retain children with a younger group. All parents believe their children deserve to be moved ahead.)

Problem: A couple doesn't enjoy the group that the bulletin defines as the one where they "belong." They feel uncomfortable about going to a class for a different category of people, even though some of their best friends are in that group.

Solution: Explain that the class descriptions are guidelines, not limits. Their purpose is to assist new people in identifying a group in which they will find common ground. Descriptions also give each group a segment of the congregation and community on which to focus outreach efforts. Individuals are encouraged to find the group in which they feel most comfortable and in which they sense the greatest potential for growth and ministry.

Problem: A boy is a year older than most others in his grade. He wants to be with kids his own age rather than his own grade.

Solution: Based on the preceding examples, one might expect to be told that the boy should be free to pick whichever group he wants. Not necessarily. Here's a time when it is important to look beyond the immediate and consider the long-term implications. Allowing a child to move ahead of his grade level may seem like the best option now, but problems can loom ahead in the middle school and high school years. Unless the child is significantly out-of-step with the rest of the group at that grade level (i.e.,

the only boy among all girls, the only athlete among a class of computer nerds, etc.), it is usually better in the long run for school-age children and youth to remain in the group for their grade.

With all other things being equal (what do you think?), a learner is better served in a group he/she has chosen than in a group he/she does not like.

Definition of Terms

Class: A group of learners with one or two teachers working together on the same lesson.

Department: A group of learners with three or more teachers working together. One of the teachers provides leadership (department leader, department superintendent, lead teacher). Part of each session usually involves some time in smaller class groupings.

Division: A major age level grouping consisting of the classes and departments that follow the same basic teaching and organizational plans. The four major divisions follow:
- Early Childhood (Birth to Age 6)
- Children (Grades 1-6)
- Youth (Grades 6-12)
- Adult (Ages 18 and up)

Follow the dominant pattern of the schools in your area to determine the age and grade limits of each division. As the number of departments grow, create new divisions (usually no more than four to six departments per division). For example:
- Babies & Toddlers (Birth to two years)
- Preschool (two to four years)
- Kindergarten (four to six years)

(*Chapter 7 has information on the staff responsibilities for each level of organization.*)

Early Childhood

All of the positive learning elements listed in the previous chapter will be very difficult, if not impossible, for teachers to provide for young children unless some basic guidelines are followed when organizing groups of children. It does not take a great deal of experience with young children to recognize the wisdom in God's plan to have the overwhelming majority of human children come into this world one at a time. While many species of animals succeed in having and raising litters of young ones, the unique nature and needs of young human beings require a high degree of personal attention. Just because it is possible to cram a large number of youngsters into one room does not mean it is desirable. A church that truly cares about providing loving, quality nurture for little ones will put a high priority on organizing its ministries for this age group so that effective learning experiences really can be provided.

Two sets of statistics tell the tale: Maximum group size and teacher-to-child ratio. If the numbers of children exceed one or both of these limits, behavior problems will increase significantly, and learning efficiency will decrease similarly. At the same time, the skill and effort needed on the part of the teachers increases with each additional child above the limits shown on page 83. While some teachers may be able to handle groups larger than those indicated, effective ministry with young children requires more than merely "handling" them. Young children need loving, personal attention far more than they need a skilled performance by a master storyteller, a gifted puppeteer, or even a musically talented clown who juggles while reciting Bible verses.

When leading a ministry for young children, it is not always possible to fully control these sets of numbers. A teacher's absence can send the teacher-to-child ratio soaring. Few leaders have the luxury of enforcing the group size standards imposed by most states on kindergartens and preschools. It is very unlikely that a teacher will block the doorway to a classroom and announce, "Sorry, we can only accept twelve children in this room. You're number thirteen. Try coming earlier next Sunday." Instead, we keep packing them in, and church leaders wonder why it is so difficult to get people to volunteer for this "duty."

These numbers should constantly remind leaders of the quality of program that young children need, nudging them away from settling for the status quo. And for teachers, these numbers can be reassuring, helping them understand that many behavior problems are caused, not by the orneriness of children, nor by the teacher's lack of skill, but by the difficult conditions that result from overcrowding or understaffing. Also, teachers must be made aware that under crowded conditions, some learning activities may need to be modified (e.g., use crayons instead of paints) or eliminated.

The key issue in maintaining optimum teacher-to-child ratios is not simply having enough big bodies in the room to keep all the little bodies under control. Of far greater importance is the need for each child to have a teacher or leader who is getting to know him/her personally, building a significant relationship, and praying regularly for that child's unique, individual growth. This type of personal attention is simply not possible when teachers have large numbers of children in their care. When the teacher-to-child ratios are exceeded, most teachers feel they're doing well just to send a birthday card and an occasional absentee note.

When Should Young Children Be Promoted?

If the sign on the door says "2's and 3's," you can be sure that parents will be bringing their little darlings to that room as soon after the second birthday as possible. Unfortunately, allowing or encouraging parents to move their children when a milestone occurs is not in the best interest of the child. Several factors should be considered in deciding when to advance children.

1. Is there room in the next group? A child is always better off staying in a less-crowded younger group than moving into an overcrowded older group.

2. Are the teachers ready? Introducing a new child who is younger than others in the group can significantly impact the dynamics of the group. Teachers may need to make significant adjustments in their session plans to accommodate the new arrival.

3. Is the child ready? Parents and teachers are often unaware (until the screaming starts) of how traumatic it can be for a young child to be taken from a familiar room into a place full of strangers. Great care needs to be taken in preparing a young child to meet new teachers and friends.

It is usually best for the child to have regularly scheduled promotion times when several children at a time can move together. Whether annually, semi-annually, quarterly, or monthly, promotion times should involve alerting teachers about the children who will be moving up so they can make advance contact with children and parents and plan for a smooth transition.

Children

Older children can adjust to larger groups better than younger children can. In some situations, these children even enjoy being part of a crowd. While it is sometimes possible to entertain and even instruct large groups of children, it is virtually impossible to build life-changing relationships with children without close personal contact.

The same two sets of statistics used with younger children apply in teaching elementary-age children: Maximum group size and teacher-to-child ratio. Children in Grades 1 and 2 need a higher level of teacher guidance than do older children, because they are beginning to cope with the challenges of using their beginning reading and writing skills. As children get older, the specific numbers vary slightly but the principles remain the same. If the teaching objective of the church involves making a lasting impact on the understanding, attitudes, and values of children, no shortcuts are available. Children require and deserve the opportunity to learn God's truth from someone they know personally and who knows and cares for them. Grouping guidelines for children are on page 84.

Every leader of children knows these numbers are not a cut-and-dried formula to be followed slavishly. Numbers rarely balance out evenly among different grade levels. Every church has at least one group with a seeming abundance of children, while the next group is noticeably sparse. However, having guidelines to follow helps ensure that adequate provision is made, not just for the children now attending, but for those the church desires to reach.

Two difficult grouping problems exist: What to do when the group is very small and what to do when the group exceeds the available staff or rooms.

When the attendance is very small, one important key is to not make the ones who came feel guilty about those who did not. A teacher with a positive attitude who communicates genuine interest and love for those who are present can make each child feel special.

When there are consistently too many children for too few adults, a frequent tendency is to tailor the type of program to accommodate the understaffed situation: "It's too hard to get enough teachers. Let's show a video to all forty of them." Sadly, such concessions tend to establish a "we can get by" mentality, making it harder to raise the congregation's awareness of what really makes a quality ministry to children. Frequently, programs that seek to work around a teacher shortage will compensate with a great array of attention-grabbing gimmicks. As a result, many people begin to equate gimmicks with quality: "It must be a good program. The kids sure like it."

While there is a place for gimmicks and excitement and "just plain fun" in any children's ministry, leaders must always be aware that no one has ever come up with a substitute for loving, Christ-like personal attention for each child.

Youth

Youth classes, especially Sunday school classes, have traditionally followed one of two grouping patterns: Plan "V" or Plan "G".

Plan "V" is followed when one or more lay *volunteers* lead one or more groups. These groups are usually divided by grade level because that enables the volunteers to maintain some semblance of control. This plan is most commonly used with middle school and/or junior high groups.

Plan "G" is followed when a youth leader ("the *Guru*") gets all youth together in the largest group possible. This plan is most commonly used with high school groups since churches are likely to assign a youth director or youth pastor to work directly with high schoolers.

The decision of how many adolescents to group together before forming an additional group is not an easy one, nor is it one that youth leaders and educators all agree on. Is it better to maintain small groups with a close teacher-to-learner ratio? Or, is it better to encourage the group to get larger under the leadership of a dynamic personality and skilled communicator?

If groups are kept small, learners may get ample personal attention and feel a sense of accountability, but many of the social dynamics that attract teenagers may be limited. A small group of teens may get to know one another and their leader very well. But teenagers, being who they are, give no guarantee they will all like each other. Instead, it is a good statistical probability that at least one young person in any group will actively dislike the others and will experience ostracism in return.

In contrast, when a group grows, so does the likelihood that young people will find someone in the group with whom they identify. Unfortunately, this someone may end up being a negative influence. Rebels and misfits usually find others of their ilk and can draw one another further away from active involvement in the group. This tendency can produce serious problems when young people are "lost in the crowd," not receiving personal attention and support from committed Christians. Grouping guidelines for youth are on page 85.

Rather than debate the pros and cons of large group vs. small groups, most successful youth ministries seek to maintain a healthful measure of both in the planning of their total ministries. Some do this by having the "official" youth leader conduct some sessions (i.e., Sunday school, Sunday evening youth group) with all the teenagers (at least all the high schoolers) together. Then, the youth leader and/or volunteers lead a variety of small group (discipleship, leadership, etc.) activities at other times.

Other youth leaders seek to accomplish the balance between small and large groups within specific programs. For example, during Sunday school, high schoolers spend part of the session in a single group led by the youth director or an experienced volunteer. At times during the same session, small groups are formed, each often guided by a volunteer leader, to engage in a specific learning activity. This balanced plan works well with groups of up to forty learners. It provides teenagers with the benefits of both small and large group experiences, even if some teens only attend that one session during the week. For example:

- Providing both small group and large group arrangements in a session allows teens to get involved personally in the learning process and to enjoy presentations for the large group.
- Small group options allow young people to get to know others well. Using small groups within the framework of a large group provides additional relationship opportunities.
- Moving between large and small groupings in a session provides variety and helps prevent boredom.
- Training volunteers is aided by their shared participation with one or more other teachers and leaders during a session.

(*Chapter 9 has additional information on small group ministries.*)

Because teenagers are so strongly influenced by peers and are so anxious to be accepted by them, the teen years are a prime time of life for reaching people for Christ and the church. Making your church's youth programs into times when young people find friendship, support, guidance, and fun are the prime considerations in deciding how to organize things. The numbers above are useful guidelines, but the specific circumstances and personality of any youth group may give reason to modify the plan.

Q: A small church has about ten teens. Should the teens meet together in one youth class or be divided into a high school and a junior high (or middle school) class?

A: It depends. If they are evenly spread from Grade 6 or 7 to Grade 12, two groups are usually preferred. The wide differences between sixth or seventh graders and twelfth graders makes it difficult to meet the needs of that great an age range. However, if the majority are high schoolers with only one or two younger students, a single class might be the best option. It should probably focus on the high school majority, but extensive personal attention should be given to the younger ones. In contrast, if the situation were reversed and all but one or two of the learners were in junior high, two groups would be preferable since most high school students do not enjoy attending a group dominated by junior high kids.

Q: When some of the ninth graders are in high school and some are in junior high, how should the church decide how to group them?

A: In general, it is much easier to put some junior high ninth graders into the high school group (they'll think they are big stuff) than it is to put some high school ninth graders back into the junior high group. Even better, if you have enough ninth graders, is to form a group just for them.

Q: What can we do when the girls in the group seem to be going on twenty-five and the boys are still chasing lizards and making obnoxious noises with their armpits?

A: First, try very hard not to laugh, even though the relative maturity levels of younger adolescent boys and girls is incongruous and sometimes hilarious. One oft-maligned approach (called old-fashioned by some) is to conduct some parts of your youth ministry with boys and girls separate. For example, in a Sunday school class where the maturity differences are obvious (middle school and junior high), at least some of the time, divide into same-sex small groups, with same-sex teachers leading the groups. Even with older teens, periodically plan separate activities for boys and girls. "Guys Night Out" and "Girls Only Event" are appealing titles for such activities. Above all, make sure that both men and women are involved in leadership, building relationships, and providing positive models for teens.

Adult

- Should adults be grouped by age or by interest?
- Should a church provide adult Sunday school or home groups?
- Should single adults and married adults be grouped together or separately?
- Should adult groups be kept small or allowed to grow?

- When should new adult groups be started?
- How can adult groups meet the needs of established Christians, new believers, as well as seekers?

Ask these questions in just about any church and watch for lively discussion. Everyone has an opinion and feels perfectly justified in expounding a viewpoint since anyone can claim to be an expert on what's good for adults on the basis of actually being an adult.

Before answering these questions, let's think about a few guidelines for grouping adults in an educational ministry. In light of the objectives set for your adult ministry, what issues need to be considered in devising a plan for grouping adults?

Every adult ministry must provide the following:

- A place for every adult—a place where all adults will feel they belong without creating tight-knit cliques;
- Opportunities for personal spiritual growth (learning) and service to others;
- A means of incorporating new people (including seekers and new believers) into the life of the congregation;
- A balance of commonality (which attracts people to one another) and variety (which challenges people to avoid stagnating) among the participants in each group.

Now let's try to answer the questions posed at the start of this section on adults. The first four questions each pose differing options which, at first glance, seem to be mutually exclusive:

- Should adults be grouped by age or by interest?

- Should a church provide adult Sunday school or home groups?
- Should single adults and married adults be grouped together or separately?
- Should adult groups be kept small or be allowed to grow?

A second glance should lead us to recognize that each of those questions should really lead us to a both/and instead of either/or approach to adult ministry.

Adults need both age level and interest groups.

Often, the two are the same, for throughout the stages of adult life, many of our deepest interests are commonly shared by people of a similar age. (Sometimes the age of the adults' family is an equally strong indicator of common interests. Parents of preschoolers share a strong bond as do parents of teenagers and adult children of aged parents.) Even if two adults share little or nothing in common as far as careers, family, Bible knowledge, or intellect, being of a similar age is a starting point to finding or to building shared experiences and interests. Thus, some method of grouping adults by age, far from being an arbitrary, unthinking assemblage, is one of the better ways of bringing together people with similar interest and experiences, especially for groups that intend to continue for an extended period of time.

Most other methods of grouping by interest tend to meet short-term needs of adults. A group of people drawn by an interest in a particular topic rarely feel drawn to continue meeting together once that topic has been explored.

Adult groups tend to grow more rapidly and consistently when they are homogeneous in some easily recognized ways. People feel more comfortable inviting

friends to a group where they feel those friends will "fit in." And visitors tend to feel less threatened in a group made up of people they immediately identify as "my kind of people."

Adults need opportunities for both Sunday school and home study group experiences.

Adult Sunday school classes have long contributed a variety of significant and fairly unique benefits.

Adult classes provide an intermediate-sized group for fellowship and mutual support since they are larger than home groups and are smaller than the total congregation. While no one can establish deep relationships with everyone in an adult class, those relationships can be built with some of those people. Most people find it easier to connect with other people in a class-sized group than in the larger congregation.

Adult classes can provide an easy "drop-in" opportunity for people whose schedules do not allow commitment to a regular schedule of meetings, or who do not feel ready to make such a commitment.

Adult classes tend to offer regular interaction with a cross-section of people, enabling participants to grow and serve.

Because adult classes meet in conjunction with the worship service, usually the week's largest gathering of the congregation, adult classes provide a natural bridge between attendance at worship and involvement in learning and fellowship.

Small groups (usually no larger than twelve) of adults meeting in homes fill a variety of important needs in the life of individuals and the church as a whole.

The informality of a home setting eases people's efforts to build and strengthen personal relationships.

Home groups can be effective out-reach vehicles since people who are reluctant to attend a church service may be open to participating in a small home group, especially with friends they already know.

Participants in small groups tend to be less inhibited about asking questions that they might not raise in a larger class.

Being in a home instead of the church building is often helpful in linking faith to daily living.

Many churches find that establishing small home groups within the framework of adult Sunday school classes achieves the benefits of both without some of their weaknesses.

Adult classes tend to be more focused on ministering to those already attending church than in reaching out to the unchurched. Establishing small home groups is an effective way to encourage class members to reach out to neighbor-hood friends.

Small groups tend to become isolated from the rest of the congregation. People who are brought into a small group are often uncomfortable with the large church service, especially if it is focused at serving Christians. Small groups within an adult class find that the class's activities and meetings are an effective bridge between the small group and the larger church family.

In addition to meeting in homes, the small groups can meet together for parts of the Sunday school class session. Also, adults benefit when a class divides ran-domly into small groups for specific learn-ing activities.

Adults benefit from time spent with those whose marital status is similar, and also with those whose status is different.

Most single adults resent attempts to "banish" them from the company of married adults, but they also experience times when being with other singles is more comfortable.

Some married adults feel awkward or threatened by some singles, especially those they perceive as possible rivals.

All churches have people who are married everywhere else in life, but are single at church because their spouses do not attend (or are involved up to the eye-balls with middle schoolers and are never seen in polite adult company).

Churches that provide groups for singles find they meet a great need. They welcome singles who do not desire to join any other group or class. Adult groups that seek to involve both married and single people need to cultivate an aware-ness of the differing needs of those they want to reach.

Adult groups need a plan for accommo-dating growth without losing their per-sonal touch.

Leaders of both Sunday school classes and home groups need to look ahead carefully to ensure that the group contin-ues to succeed.

Groups tend to have their greatest growth in the first eighteen months of existence. Long-established groups rarely grow much.

Once a group reaches an attendance plateau, it is more likely to maintain that level or decline than it is to begin a new period of growth.

New leadership or a new nucleus of people committed to growth can produce growth in an established group.

In order to sustain attendance growth among adults, it is usually more effective to start one or more new groups while enthusiasm is high than to allow existing groups to grow until they plateau.

A new adult group needs a committed nucleus willing to expend time and energy to make the group attractive and purposeful.

When starting a new group, it is important that those in the original group are left with capable leaders who are motivated to continue growing.

Grouping guidelines for adults are on pages 87 and 88.

A worksheet on effective adult grouping is on pages 89 and 90.

Grouping Guidelines for Early Childhood

Mark the blanks to rate your present grouping for early childhood.

E=Excellent
S=Satisfactorily
Doing Now
I=Improvement Needed
N=Need to Start

A new department should be formed whenever an existing department approaches maximum group size and/or room capacity.

The maximum group sizes assume that the rooms are large enough to accommodate that number of children (Chapter 7) and that enough teachers are involved to maintain the proper teacher-to-child ratios. If the ratio of children to teachers is higher than the number listed, the maximum group size must decrease in proportion.

	Age	Maximum Group Size	Teacher:Learner Ratio
____	1. Ages 0 to 12 mo.	10-12	1:2
____	2. Ages 12 to 24 mo.	12-15	1:2
____	3. Ages 2 to 3 years	14-16	1:3
____	4. Ages 4 to 6 years	16-20	1:4

As Your Early Childhood Division Grows

# of Children	Grouping	Staff
1-8	**One Department** Birth to Age 6	Two Teachers
6-30	**Two Departments** Birth to Age 2 1/2 Ages 2 1/2 - 6	Two Department Leaders Two to Five Teachers
25-50	**Three Departments** Birth to Age 2 Ages 2-3 Ages 4-6	Three Department Leaders Three to Ten teachers
45-80	**Four or Five Departments** Babies Toddlers Age 2 Ages 3-4 Ages 5-6	Four or Five Department Leaders Five to Sixteen Teachers
75-110	**Six Departments** Babies Toddlers Age 2 Age 3 Age 4 Ages 5-6	Six Department Leaders Six to Twenty-two Teachers
100-200	**Twelve Departments** Babies/Babies Toddlers/Toddlers Age 2/Age 2 Age 3/Age 3 Age 4/Age 4 Ages 5-6/Ages 5-6	Twelve Department Leaders Twelve to Forty Teachers

Grouping Guidelines for Children

Mark the blanks to rate your present grouping for children.

E=Excellent
S=Satisfactorily Doing Now
I=Improvement Needed
N=Need to Start

	Grades	Maximum Group Size	Teacher:Learner Ratio
____	1. Grades 1, 2	20-25	1:6
____	2. Grades 3-6	25-30	1:8

A new class or department should be formed whenever an existing department approaches maximum group size and/or room capacity.

The maximum group sizes assume that the rooms are large enough to accommodate that number of children (Chapter 7) and that enough teachers are involved to maintain the proper teacher-to-child ratios. If the ratio of children to teachers is higher than the number listed, the maximum group size must decrease in proportion.

As Your Children's Division Grows

# of Children	Grouping	Staff
1-10	**One Class** Grades 1-5 or 6	One or Two Teachers
8-20	**Two Classes** Grades 1-2 Grades 3-5 or 6	Two to Four Teachers
16-32	**Two Departments of Two Classes Each** Grades 1-2/Grades 3-5 or 6 Grades 1-2/Grades 3-5 or 6	Two Department Leaders Two to Four Teachers
30-60	**Three Departments of Two or Three Classes Each** Grades 1-2/Grades 3-4 Grades 1-2/Grades 3-4 Grades 5-6/Grades 5-6s	Three Department Leader Five to Eight Teachers
50-100	**Four or Five Departments of Two to Four Classes Each** Grade 1/Grade 2 Grade 1/Grade 2 Grade 3/Grade 4 Grade 3/Grade 4 Grades 5-6/Grades 5-6	Four or Five Department Leaders Six to Twelve Teachers

Sixth graders should usually be grouped at church as they are in your local schools. If most of your sixth graders attend elementary school, keep them in the children's division. But if most of them are in middle school, then they should be with the middle schoolers in your church.

Grouping Guidelines for Youth

Mark the blanks to rate your present grouping for youth.

E=Excellent
S=Satisfactorily
Doing Now
I=Improvement Needed
N=Need to Start

A new class or department should be formed whenever an existing department approaches maximum group size and/or room capacity.

The maximum group size assumes that a room is large enough to accommodate that number of young people (Chapter 8) and that enough teachers and leaders are involved to maintain effective teacher-to-learner ratios. If the ratio of teens to teachers is higher than the number listed, the maximum group size should decrease in proportion. When the maximum group size is exceeded, the leader can no longer be personally involved with all learners. Even if there are enough adults to maintain the teacher-to-learner ratio, each additional teacher makes the logistics of training and guiding staff increasingly complex, further reducing the leader's time spent with learners.

Grouping Guidelines for Youth

Youth	Maximum Group Size	Teacher:Learner Ratio
____ Grades 6-12	30-40	1:8

As Your Youth Division Grows

# of Youth	Grouping	Staff
1-10	**One Class** Grades 6 or 7 - 12	One or Two Teachers
8-80	**Two Departments/Classes** Grades 6 or 7 - 8 or 9 Grades 9 or 10 - 12	Two Leaders Two to Eight Teachers
60-120	**Three Departments/Classes** Grades 6 or 7 - 8 Grades 9 - 10 Grades 11 - 12	Five to Twelve Teachers Three Leaders
100-200	**Four or Five Departments** Grade 6 and/or 7 Grade 8 Grade 9 Grade 10 Grades 11-12	Four or Five Leaders Eight to Twenty Teachers

Sixth and ninth graders should usually be grouped at church as they are in your local schools. If most of your ninth graders attend high school, group them with the high schoolers. But if most of them are in junior high, that's where they should be in your church.

The above numbers are based on a balanced program in which a youth leader or skilled volunteer leads parts of the session in a large group, and other parts of the session involve small groups (up to eight per group), with a leader available for each group.

Effective Adult Grouping

Rate your present plan for grouping adults in terms of how well it provides these elements:

E=Excellent
S=Satisfactorily
     Doing Now
I=Improvement Needed
N=Need to Start

Elements of Grouping

_____ 1. Adult classes provide a place for every adult—a place where adults feel they belong without creating tight-knit cliques.

_____ 2. Adult classes provide opportunity for personal spiritual growth (learning) and service to others.

_____ 3. Adult classes provide a means of incorporating new people (including seekers and new believers) into the life of the congregation.

_____ 4. Adult classes provide a healthy balance of commonality (which attracts people to one another) and variety (which challenges people to avoid stagnating) among the participants in each group.

_____ 5. _____

_____

Adult Sunday school classes have long contributed a variety of significant and fairly unique benefits. Rate your church's adult classes in meeting these needs:

Benefits of Grouping

_____ 1. Adult classes provide an intermediate-size group for fellowship and mutual support since they are larger than home groups and are smaller than the total congregation. While no one can establish deep relationships with everyone in an adult class, such relationships can be built with some of those people. Most people find it easier to connect with other people in a class-size group than in the larger congregation.

_____ 2. Adult classes provide an easy "drop-in" opportunity for people whose schedules do not allow commitment to a regular schedule of meetings, or who do not feel ready to make such a commitment.

_____ 3. Adult classes offer regular interaction with a cross-section of people, enabling participants to grow and serve.

_____ 4. Because adult classes meet in conjunction with the worship service, usually the week's largest gathering of the congregation, adult classes provide a natural bridge between attendance at worship and involvement in learning and fellowship.

_____ 5. _____

_____

Small groups (usually no larger than twelve) of adults meeting in homes fill a variety of important needs in the life of individuals and the church as a whole. Rate your church's small groups in meeting these needs:

Small Groups

_____ 1. The informality of a home setting helps people build and strengthen personal relationships.

_____ 2. Home groups can be effective outreach vehicles since people who are reluctant to attend a church service may be open to participating in a small home group, especially with friends they already know.

_____ 3. Participants in small groups tend not to be inhibited about asking questions which they might not raise in a larger class.

_____ 4 Being in a home instead of the church building is often helpful in linking faith to daily living.

_____ 5. _____

_____

Grouping Guidelines
for Adults

Mark the blanks to rate your present grouping for adults.

E=Excellent
S=Satisfactorily
  Doing Now
I=Improvement Needed
N=Need to Start

Adults	Maximum Group Size	Leader:Learner Ratio
____ Small Home Groups	8-12[1]	1:8[2]
____ Sunday School Classes	30-40[3]	1:8[4]

[1]Small groups made up of couples continue to work well with slightly larger numbers than groups of unrelated individuals. It is easier for the leader to make contacts and build relationships with a couple than with two unrelated people. If one person in a couple is going to be absent, often the other person will, also. Thus, allowing six couples in a group provides a "cushion" against having so few people at a given session that group dynamics suffer.

[2]If a group involves more than four or five couples, it is wise to have a co-leader or host who is responsible for any hospitality related matters (refreshments, furniture, greeting people, etc.), while the group leader focuses on the group's study. This person can also assist with some of the session-leading responsibilities.

[3]This number reaches the upper limits of the number of people with whom the average person can readily build friendships. While a minority of very gregarious people can "get to know" many more people, groups that exceed these limits cease being places where people feel they know everyone. For adult classes to continue to grow and to nurture successfully the growth of everyone involved, a very strong and committed leadership is required, both in teaching, in organizing, and in maintaining contact with group members. Many very large churches intentionally build large adult classes (sometimes calling them small churches), assigning them a wide range of the church's ministry functions. Such groups are often led by church staff members as a major part of their ministry responsibility.

[4]This ratio reflects the need for adult groups to enlist and train a leadership team that provides a high degree of personal attention to group members. While many adult classes have traditionally had officers who were responsible for various class functions (missions projects, social events, etc.), the important number in effective adult ministry is to have enough leaders prepared to accept personal responsibility for up to eight adults each. These "care group" leaders may lead small group sessions during the week, or they may focus on personal contacts with the people they have been assigned. If group leaders are expected to be responsible for more than eight people, the degree of personal contacts and accountability will diminish.

(*Chapter 9 has more information about small group ministries.*)

As Your Adult Division Grows

Start a new class whenever an existing class approaches the recommended maximum size.

# of Adults	Grouping	Staff
1-25	One Class One Teacher	One to Three Group Leaders
20-60	Two Classes Young Adults (18-35) Middle & Older Adults (30+)	Two Teachers Two to Eight Group Leaders
50-120	Three or Four Classes Young Adults (18-30) Middle Adults I (25-45) Middle Adults II (40-55) Older Adults (50+)	Three or Four Teachers Six to Fourteen Group Leaders
100+	Five or More Classes Young Adults (18-30) Middle Adults I (25-35) Middle Adults II (30-45) Middle Adults III (40-55) Older Adults (50+)	At Least One Teacher per Class One Group Leader per Eight Adults

Add classes for college and singles as soon as a nucleus is available. Add short-term electives as interest or need arises. (*Chapter 5 contains information on adult electives.*)

Adjust the suggested age ranges of the groups in the chart to fit the people in the congregation. The ages are shown to overlap so that people are free to choose the group in which they feel most comfortable.

5
Alternative Models

I recall sitting in on a heated debate about a radical change in the life of our church. A proposal had been made that Sunday school begin at 9:30 instead of 9:45.

As long as anyone in our church could remember, Sunday school had always begun at 9:45. How could anyone consider tampering with such a long-standing tradition? As far as many people in our church were concerned, any church that had Sunday school at a time other than 9:45 was viewed with uneasy suspicion.

I had the feeling a few opponents of the time switch scoured their concordances looking for biblical support for keeping Sunday school in its sacred hour. And those who advocated the change were caught up in an aura that they were pioneering a remarkable innovation that would remake the face of Christian education.

As we look at the church and the Sunday school into the twenty-first century, that debate over a fifteen-minute time change appears ludicrous. The last several decades of the twentieth century produced a wide variety of changes in the schedule, format, and underlying objectives of the Sunday school.

The Sunday school used to be a ministry that most churches had in common, not just in terms of when it met (give or take fifteen minutes or so on Sunday morning), but also in terms of how its ministry was carried out. At the turn of a new century, a variety of alternate approaches compete, causing leaders to consider which options will best meet the needs of their situation.

Schedule

Differing time schedules are among the most obvious variations in the way churches provide educational ministries. Some time schedule variations resulted as an attempt to absorb growth that had exceeded the capacity of available facilities, while other options were tried due to a decline in attendance. Other approaches resulted from efforts to reach out to people who might not respond as easily to traditional programs, while some were implemented as a convenience to those already attending.

Multiple Sessions

Large churches may offer more than one session of Sunday school. They may do this because they have enough people to offer some groups two or more times. Some churches offer multiple sessions because it would be difficult to fit everyone who attends into a single session.

In many cases, these churches offer groups for all ages at each session. In other cases, some groups meet only at one designated session. It is not uncommon for churches with two sessions to offer a middle school program one hour and a high school program at another hour, both using the same room. A single adult group, or a young married class, or a particular adult elective may meet at only one hour.

Churches can and do succeed with multiple session programs, but only if they consistently promote the program to encourage people to attend. In addition, they usually find they must work harder than with a single program to build and maintain personal relationships and a sense of belonging.

Simultaneous Sessions

Another schedule variation offers Sunday school simultaneously with the worship service or some other program (e.g., choir practice). Many churches schedule two or more programs at once to accommodate busy families. This enables adults to participate in one type of program while their children or youth are involved in another at the same time.

Churches with multiple Sunday school sessions and worship services that meet simultaneously usually encourage people to attend both programs. Churches with a single session intend for everyone to participate in just the one program offered for their age group (i.e., adults and teens attend worship, children attend Sunday school). In attempting to accomplish everything in one session, some churches extend the length of that session. Others, divide the session, at least for children, having them spend part of the time with the adults (i.e., in worship) and the rest of the time in a children's program (i.e., Sunday school). (*See the "Children and Youth Only" option in the "Grouping" section later in this chapter.*)

Churches struggle to find the right balance between making their programs "user-friendly" to the unchurched while at the same time challenging their members to meaningful growth in the Christian life. Part of this struggle involves trying to determine how much time each week people should be encouraged to devote to corporate worship, learning, and fellowship. Following are some of the questions that need to be discussed by church leaders.

• With one hundred and sixty-eight hours available each week, is one hour on Sunday morning adequate to minister effectively to people's needs?

- Does adding one hour each week make a significant difference in people's lives?
- Can more people be enlisted in a program of consistent learning and growth if it is scheduled immediately before or after an event they are already attending (i.e., Sunday worship service) or if it is scheduled at a different day or time?
- Does the church have a strategy for helping people move from minimal commitment to a deeper level of involvement?

Alternate Times

Besides the schedule options mentioned above, many churches have successfully experimented with offering Sunday school at a time other than Sunday morning. In many cases, moving Sunday school to another day or time of the week has led to using a different name. But whatever it may be called, churches are reaching people through Sunday schools that meet at the following times:

- Sunday afternoons or evenings (very common among ethnic congregations that share a facility)
- Saturday nights
- Saturday mornings
- Weeknights
- Weekday afternoons

Because our society has moved away from respecting Sunday as a day of reverence, many people experience an appealing sense of balancing the scales by moving Sunday school sessions into time slots once viewed as primarily secular. Most churches that offer Sunday school at other times of the week do so in addition to their Sunday morning Sunday school.

Some make it their only Sunday school. In either case, the scheduling is usually determined by a desire to reach people who have made Sundays their day of recreation instead of reverence.

Weighing the pros and cons of change can be disturbing to many people, especially those who treasure their church involvement as a constant in a rapidly shifting world. However, people who take seriously Christ's instructions to reach out must be willing to move beyond what is comfortable and actively embrace changes that are needed in order to win people not currently being reached. Careful consideration of items in the "disadvantages" list is necessary so that leaders and people are truly prepared to implement change without creating casualties.

Grouping

Children and Youth Only

The discussion above about simultaneous sessions touched on a plan that offer Sunday school only for children and/or youth, with no adult classes. Some churches that have Sunday school preceding or following worship have eliminated adult classes. Chapter 1 mentioned that a children-only program has been the dominant pattern of Sunday school in England since the days of Robert Raikes. Now, as we move into the new century, this option is seen in a variety of formats and for a variety of reasons.

- In some churches, adult classes became so boring, no one wanted to attend, so they were dropped.
- The high cost of land and construction has forced many new and growing churches into using warehouse or

commercial property. In many of these cases, space for adult classes has simply not been available.

• In other cases, church leaders have intentionally chosen not to invest in space for adult classes, using funds for other purposes.

• Some church leaders who sought to penetrate their communities abandoned adult Sunday school as fostering an "in-grown" mentality, serving those who already attend rather than being a means of reaching out to the unchurched.

• Some leaders focus their attention on home groups to the exclusion of adult classes.

• Some churches have chosen to have lengthy worship services with the pastor providing the teaching for everyone, rather than having lay teachers leading adult classes.

While some churches have been successful with a children- and/or youth-only Sunday school, unfortunately, very few churches have been able to compensate fully for the loss of strong, active adult Bible classes. No other ministry has succeeded on a broad scale to involve, instruct, and equip as many adults on a regular basis, while providing a stable framework for teaching children and youth. It is no surprise when a church reestablishes adult Sunday school classes in order to regain the many benefits they provide.

Large Groups

One of the hallmarks of the Sunday school has long been its structure of small groups in which personal attention and strong relationships have been built. While some adult and youth classes were allowed to grow quite large, they tended to be seen as more of the exception rather than the rule, often reflecting the leadership of a highly skilled and dynamic teacher. The mainstream Sunday schools, especially at the children's level, have historically been dominated by small classes.

However, some churches have moved almost totally away from a small-group oriented Sunday school, opting for large groups. Reasons for this shift include the following:

• It has become increasingly difficult to enlist and train capable teachers. Thus, some churches have opted to focus on developing relatively few teachers who can each lead a large group rather than preparing a larger number of teachers who each lead a small group.

• The high cost of facilities has led some churches to move away from providing the number of rooms needed for smaller groups. Fewer, larger rooms are less costly to build, equip, and maintain.

• Many church leaders feel more comfortable and successful leading a large class than they do enlisting, training, and supporting a team of volunteers to guide numerous smaller groups successfully. The most recognized model of Christian teaching is that of the preacher speaking to a large group. Relatively few church leaders are skilled in using, let alone training others to use, the interactive teaching methods that make small groups so effective.

• Large classes, especially at the youth and adult levels, can generate enthusiasm that many smaller groups do not.

Bigger is not necessarily better, especially in the vital process of nurturing people in the Christian life. Jesus, the Master

Teacher, spent more time with the twelve than with the multitudes. His most memorable teachings were presented while interacting with individuals (the rich young ruler, Nicodemus, the woman at the well, etc.). Saying this in no way negates the attraction or impact of Jesus' ministry to large crowds, but it does recognize the need in the church for a balance between large group proclamation and worship and small group interaction and accountability.

Unfortunately, some churches model their Sunday school after their worship service, providing a large percentage of their people with two very similar programs, rather than a balanced diet. The power of the personal touch can get lost.

It gets lost when programs become performance oriented rather than person centered. For example, large children's programs that feature puppets or clowns or magic or other communication devices may be highly entertaining and instructive. However, the "performers" may never interact directly with the children and as a result, the children learn to think of themselves as the "audience" rather than members of the church.

It gets lost when communication is a one-way street, rather than a process of give and take. When we see how often Jesus' closest followers misunderstood the things he said to the crowds, it is very clear why Jesus often followed his public teaching with times of question and answer with the twelve (Mark 4:1-10; 10:1-10).

It gets lost when the teacher is not close enough to the learners to observe their growth. Large groups tend to foster anonymity rather than accountability unless there is accompanying opportunity for interaction within a small group.

Intergenerational Groups

When we succeed in getting a contemporary family to come to the same place at the same time, why do we split them up until it's time to leave? Why does the Sunday school pull families apart?

During the last half of the twentieth century, the church has wrestled with how to strengthen beleaguered families. Since today's families tend to attend church less frequently than was the practice a generation or two ago, many church leaders asked, "Could we better use that time to strengthen families?" The idea of grouping people by age took on a somewhat sinister aspect, and churches experimented with bringing families together instead of family members all going to their own classes.

Numerous healthy lessons were learned through these experiments.

- A great deal of difference exists between a two-year-old, a twelve-year-old, and everyone over twenty-two.
- Trying to find something that all ages enjoy doing together is not simple. Even eating is not an easily shared experience when youngsters crave sugar and adults want decaf and low-cal.
- When a topic and an activity clicks with all ages, it's exciting! When a topic or an activity does not appeal to all ages, it can be very painful for everyone.
- Teenagers and older children tend to look down on anything that younger children enjoy. Teenagers also tend to look down on anything that their parents enjoy. All of which means, involving young people in intergenerational learning experiences is about as

difficult as getting them to visit with their aunts and uncles at a family reunion.

- Intergenerational learning experiences work best as short-term changes of pace, rather than as the ongoing structure. Retreats, camps, Vacation Bible School, and other limited-time programs can provide very effective opportunities for families to learn together.
- Peer group classes, rather than family classes, offer families a vital type of support. Sunday school teachers are powerful allies, offering children and young people the support of friendly, caring adults who are not their parents.

Additional Needs to Consider

Anyone who has ever served in a church is well aware that organizing any ministry would be easier if it weren't for all the people who defy attempts to classify them. No matter how a church chooses to organize itself for its teaching, nurturing ministries, it will always need groups that do not fit within the standard organizational plan.

Exceptional Learners

Most churches wait to confront the unique needs of exceptional learners when someone within the church has a physical, mental, or emotional disability. Typically, the church will try to accommodate this person within an existing group. If it becomes difficult for this learner to progress with others of the same age, he/she may then be placed with younger learners. At some point this may no longer be in the best interests of the learner or of the other children, so the church begins to explore the possibility of a special class.

In most cases, one person within the church will take the initiative to explore the possibility of starting a special class. To the surprise of everyone (except the parents of the special learner), most churches quickly discover new prospects for a ministry to those with special needs. News about this class quickly spreads through the well-established network of special-need families, and people are drawn to a church that shows it truly cares.

Two major (and related) difficulties in such a group are the widely differing mental and physical abilities of learners and the scarcity of resources that target those abilities. Teachers need to be highly flexible, ready to adapt available materials to individual needs.

Seekers, New Believers, New Members Classes

Sooner or later, most Christian groups start thinking first of the needs of those already in the church rather than the needs of those yet to be reached. Thus, most Sunday school classes, especially at the youth and adult levels, find it difficult to provide instruction that meets the needs of long-term Christians as well as novices in the faith.

Any church that is serious about winning the unchurched must give careful consideration to how it will go about teaching and nurturing those it reaches. Two major approaches should be carried out simultaneously through the Sunday school and other educational ministries.

First, all Sunday school classes should be continually challenged to evaluate their efforts to incorporate new people. This must involve not just welcoming people who transfer from other churches, but actively pursuing steps to help seekers and new believers feel loved and accepted. Every lesson must be looked at from the perspective of those who have little or no biblical or theological background. Some people fear this could make everything so basic that long-term Christians will be bored. On the contrary, the fresh viewpoint of people who have not learned the jargon or safe answers can be like a breath of fresh air to any group willing to put the needs of newcomers ahead of the desires of the "old guard."

Second, the church should conduct either periodic or ongoing classes for seekers and new believers.

Periodic classes start at least once each year. Participants continue through the duration of the course. This plan allows a group to grow together, and content can build on what was studied in previous sessions.

Ongoing classes run continuously. People start at any time and continue until they complete all the sessions. Thus, an interested person does not have to wait until a new class starts.

The objective of these classes is to provide an essential foundation in the basics of the Christian faith. They provide the opportunity for people to affirm their faith in Christ. Upon completion, participants are guided into a new members class followed by continued involvement in the regular classes available.

Seeker and new believer classes tend to last from four to thirteen weeks. A new class should be started as often as possible to avoid having to tell someone, "It's good that you're interested in learning what it means to be a Christian, but we won't have a class on that for nine more months." Many churches enlist several committed members to participate in the class in order to provide prayer and personal support for those who are new.

Youth and Adult Electives

Three main patterns exist for how youth and adult course material is chosen. Many churches have a combination of all three approaches.

1. The church (i.e., the Christian education board, a pastor, the youth director) selects a curriculum that groups will study.

2. The groups themselves (i.e., the teacher) decide what they will study.

3. People choose which group to attend based on what content they are studying.

In the first two situations, learners continue with the same group regardless of what is being studied. The challenge is to select topics that appeal to the broad range of interests, backgrounds, and personalities in any typical group and that build strong enough relationships within the group so that people will attend even when a particular topic is not of high interest to them.

In the third situation, learners stay with a group only for the duration of the topic, then they move to another group where a new topic of interest is being explored.

In order to experience the benefits of electives while minimizing the disadvantages (pages 105 and 106), it is recommended that electives be offered to supplement ongoing youth and adult groups rather than to replace them. There are various ways that this can be done.

- Offer one or more electives each quarter (or semester) while ongoing classes continue. Limit enrollment so that existing classes are not depleted. Obviously, a popular elective should be offered again so that all who want to take it may do so.
- Offer electives at another time (Sunday evening, weeknight, weekend,

retreat). This is especially effective if consistent attendance is essential. Other times of the week may have fewer conflicts than Sunday morning.

- Schedule an elective as a change of pace for a specific ongoing class. Make sure that there is high interest in the topic; then promote it heavily among the members and prospects of that group. A guest instructor may be used or the regular teacher may lead.

- Schedule an elective term at sometime during the year (e.g., summer, January) when all or most regular classes take a break and people are encouraged to choose from the elective offerings. During this time, especially if the electives succeed in attracting people who do not ordinarily attend the ongoing groups, the leadership of those groups must work energetically to promote attendance when their groups resume. One helpful approach is for each group to schedule a social event for their members and prospects during the elective term.

- For each elective offered, enlist a teacher and a nucleus of committed, involved people who will attend that elective and take responsibility for the outreach, fellowship, and service objectives. Prepare these people to ensure that all who attend will be personally welcomed, prayed for, and encouraged to build relationships and become involved in the life of the church.

Ethnic and Foreign Language Classes

Increasing ethnic diversity is one of the major changes that occurred in the closing decades of the twentieth century and that will continue into the twenty-first century.

Not only will this be a factor in major urban areas but in medium and small towns as well. In California, Caucasians—once the majority racial classification—are being outnumbered by a diverse and growing population of Asians, Hispanics, and African-Americans. As populations have shifted, many churches have found that their congregation no longer reflects the ethnic makeup of their surrounding communities.

Some churches in this situation move out of their communities. In many cases, relocating energizes a congregation and results in significant numerical growth. However, nagging doubts usually remain about the unreached people in the neighborhood left behind.

Many churches launch ministries to ethnic groups in their community. In many cases, this takes the form of allowing an ethnic congregation to use their facilities. In large part, the people and leadership of each congregation remain separate, joining together only occasionally.

Some other churches make outreach to another ethnic group part of their own responsibility. Ministry to children and young people is the most common form of such efforts, with programs including Sunday school classes, after-school programs, Vacation Bible School, and clubs. Churches that conduct outreach to ethnic groups tend to operate these ministries separately from the programs for the children and youth of their own church families.

There is no question that there is a growing mission field of people who need to be reached and taught. At present, only a small minority of evangelical churches have given serious consideration to their role in reaching these peoples.

Advantages and Disadvantages of Multiple Sessions

If you are presently offering multiple sessions, mark the advantages your church has experienced by doing so. If you are not presently offering multiple sessions, mark the advantages you think your church could experience by doing so. Add any comments to explain your marks. Add any advantages you have experienced that are not listed here.

Mark Advantages

Comments

____ More people can be accommodated than in a single session.

____ Many people enjoy having a choice of when to attend.

____ Costs can be kept in check by getting additional use out of present facilities with little or no added expense.

____ Adding a new session can be a catalyst for growth, motivating additional people to get involved in ministry and challenging people to reach out.

Mark Disadvantages

Comments

If you are presently offering multiple sessions, mark the disadvantages your church has experienced by doing so. If you are not presently offering multiple sessions, mark the disadvantages you think your church could experience by doing so. Add any comments to explain your marks. Add any disadvantages you have experienced that are not listed here.

___ Continuity and relationships can suffer as people switch back and forth between sessions.

___ People lose contact with those who usually attend a different session.

___ Some people feel less accountable to attend if their absence is less likely to be noticed than with one session.

___ Some people are less likely to agree to a continuing responsibility in one session if they like being able to switch.

___ _____

_____

Advantages and Disadvantages of Simultaneous Sessions

If you are presently offering simultaneous sessions, mark the advantages your church has experienced by doing so. If you are not presently offering simultaneous sessions, mark the advantages you think your church could experience by doing so. Add any comments to explain your marks. Add any advantages you have experienced that are not listed.

Mark Advantages   Comments

_____ It is easier to attract some people to a single session than to two separate ones.

_____ Simultaneous sessions can con serve time and resources.

_____ If attendance at one session is small, it often helps to provide only the programs most people are interested in (i.e., adult worship, children's Sunday school).

_____ When multiple sessions are provided, simultaneous Sunday school and worship may get maximum use out of facilities with minimal added cost.

_____ When both Sunday school and worship are each offered in two or more sessions, some people are easier to involve because they have the option to attend worship (or adult Sunday school) in another session.

_____

_____

Mark Disadvantages

Comments

If you are presently offering simultaneous sessions, mark the disadvantages your church has experienced by doing so. If you are not presently offering simultaneous sessions, mark the disadvantages you think your church could experience by doing so. Add any comments to explain your marks. Add any disadvantages you have experienced that are not listed.

_____ Incorporating people into the life of the church tends to be more difficult if no adult or youth groups meet in the hours adjacent to worship service.

_____ Enlisting people to serve in children's or youth programs tends to be more difficult with only one simultaneous session than when Sunday school immediately precedes or follows worship.

_____ Churches with simultaneous Sunday school and worship must consistently promote participation in adult and youth groups in order to move people beyond a "one-stop" approach to church life.

_____ Church leaders tend to focus on the one session they lead or attend, resulting in a division between those involved in worship and those involved in Sunday school.

_____ Attendance of children and young people may suffer as they notice parents and other adults not participating in similar learning groups.

_____ Churches with no Sunday morning adult groups tend to have a smaller percentage of adults involved in group learning experiences than churches that provide Sunday morning groups.

_____ Many children and young people do not make the transition to continued attendance once they outgrow the available Sunday morning groups.

Advantages and Disadvantages of Simultaneous Sessions
2

_____ _____

_____

Advantages and Disadvantages of Alternate Times

The advantages and disadvantages of meeting at another time of week are similar to those for having multiple sessions. If you are presently offering Sunday school at an alternate time(s), mark the advantages your church has experienced by doing so. If you are not presently offering Sunday school at an alternate time, mark the advantages you think your church could experience by doing so. Add any comments to explain your marks. Add any advantages you have experienced that are not listed.

Mark	Advantages	Comments
____	It is easier to attract some people to a time other than Sunday morning.	
____	Adding a session at an alternate time can enable some people to serve who could not do so on Sunday morning.	
____	If attendance at the alternate time is small, it often helps to provide only the programs most people are interested in (i.e., adult worship, children's Sunday school).	
____	Providing Sunday school at an alternate time can help get maximum use out of facilities with minimal added cost.	
____	Some churches find a weekday or night Sunday school has better continuity in attendance than Sundays, since people are not as likely to leave town then as for weekend recreation.	
____	_____	

Mark Disadvantages   Comments

If you are presently offering Sunday school at an alternate time(s), mark the disadvantages your church has experienced by doing so. If you are not presently offering Sunday school at an alternate time, mark the disadvantages you think your church could experience by doing so. Add any comments to explain your marks. Add any disadvantages you have experienced that are not listed.

____ Incorporating people into the life of the church tends to be more difficult if no adult or youth groups meet at the alternate time.

____ Enlisting people to serve in children's or youth programs for an alternate time tends to be more difficult if they must make another trip to attend worship and/or adult classes.

____ Consistency of attendance at any given session diminishes as more options are provided. When people switch when they attend from week to week, building relationships becomes very difficult, especially in children's and youth groups..

____ People who establish a pattern of attending at the alternate time tend to feel separated from those involved in worship and/or Sunday school at another time.

____ _____

_____

Advantages and Disadvantages of Offering Electives

As with most things in life, there are advantages and disadvantages to offering elective classes for youth and adults. If you are presently offering electives, mark the advantages your church has experienced by doing so. If you are not presently offering electives, mark the advantages you think your church could experience by doing so. Add any comments to explain your marks. Add any additional advantages that you have experienced that are not listed.

Mark Advantages   Comments

____ It is easier to attract some people to a topic in which they are interested than to a group with whom they have not yet established relationships.

____ Electives enable the church to provide some specialized instruction in areas that might not be appropriate or effective within existing groups.

____ If attendance in existing adult groups has stagnated, electives can generate new interest.

____ Electives provide opportunities for some people to teach who might not be drawn to teaching an ongoing group.

____ Electives offer a means for people to interact with others outside their usual groupings.

People may agree to a higher level of commitment for an elective topic than for an ongoing group.

____ _____

_____

Mark Disadvantages

Comments

If you are presently offering electives, mark the disadvantages your church has experienced by doing so. If you are not presently offering electives, mark the disadvantages you think your church could experience by doing so. Add any comments to explain your marks. Add any additional disadvantages that you have experienced that are not listed.

_____ People who attend a class on a specific topic will not necessarily continue to attend once that topic is concluded.

_____ People who are drawn to teach a particular topic are sometimes more focused on the information than on the people, thus relationships may not be built that will link people into further growth opportunities.

_____ Smaller churches may find it difficult to secure leadership for specialized elective topics or to offer a variety of topics to interest enough people.

_____ Predicting how many people will attend a particular class is difficult, often resulting in wide imbalances. While it is possible to keep groups from getting too large, it can be very discouraging to those involved in groups that end up being very small.

_____ It is difficult to establish a nucleus of leadership within an elective class so that caring and ministry needs are provided.

_____ Because electives are topic centered and of limited duration, the other objectives (outreach, fellowship, service) of ministry groups tend to be overlooked.

_____ _____

_____

_____

Advantages and Disadvantages of Offering Electives
2

6 Administration

How did you become an administrator in your church's educational ministry?"

This question was asked of a group of people who appeared normal, intelligent, and friendly. They wore big name tags. Most had lugged bulky briefcases, backpacks, carry-alls, or shopping bags into the workshop room. The question seemed to make them all nervous.

Finally, a woman ventured to answer, "I guess since I had been teaching for so long, it was the only other thing they could think of to do with me."

Nervous laughter rippled through this group of dignified leaders.

Someone else volunteered, "Someone had to do it, and no one else was willing to tackle it."

The group was starting to loosen up. Maybe it was OK to admit that they didn't all feel highly qualified, with extensive training and special leadership abilities.

"When they asked me, I couldn't think of a good reason to say no."

"I really wanted to help make a difference in our Sunday school."

"Since I spend all week on my job supervising employees, I guess they figured I knew something about administration."

"I prayed about it and for some reason, God seemed to nudge me to do it. I just figured he must know what he was doing."

People become leaders of the Sunday school, children's church, club programs, youth groups, and adult ministries for a wide variety of reasons and with equally wide variations in their background and preparation for the demands of a leadership role. While there is a vast amount of material available for what to do in teaching a class, there is relatively little help for how to lead the teachers.

Anyone having an administrative role for the Sunday school or any other educational ministry must explore the keys to effective leadership. These keys provide more than just skill and the knowledge about how others are supposed to do their jobs. Even more important, these keys include an understanding of how to build an environment of mutually supportive relationships.

Even on an assembly line where there is only one correct way to attach a widget to a thing-a-ma-bob, the effective leader must give as much attention to personal, human factors as to the specifics of each task. How much more in a ministry that seeks to help people grow and mature in Christ must leaders follow the principles and procedures that contribute to the emotional and spiritual health of all involved! Unfortunately, churches too often "burn out" their volunteers, treating them as expendable troops in battle. The result of such "volunteer abuse" is a host of casualties, many of whom withdraw from any future service and others who abandon the church completely.

Administration: A Neglected Gift

Administration is listed among the gifts the Holy Spirit has placed within the church. Along with gifts of prophecy, healing, and helping others, we read of "those with gifts of administration" (1 Corinthians 12:28). The original word used for this gift (*kubernésis*—translated "governments" in the *King James Version*) denotes the process of guiding or steering and is very different from another word (*kuriotés*—also translated "government" in 2 Peter 2:10) which denotes dominion or lordship.

Similarly, where Romans 12:8 tells those with the gift of leadership to "govern diligently," the original word (a form of *proistémi*—translated "ruleth" in the *King James Version*) literally means "to stand before" and therefore is used to indicate leading and being devoted to. The latter sense is conveyed in Titus 3:8, 14 in admonitions that people "*devote* themselves to doing what is good."

This brief look at the biblical view of administration is vital because many people have a very confused idea of what the word really means. Administration is commonly used as if it were a synonym for supervision or management. Such usage implies that an administrator is someone who makes decisions, issues directives, and basically gets people to do their jobs. While those actions may be aspects of administration, they totally miss the core of what the term really means.

Take a good look at this familiar English word.

ADMINISTRATION

Let's begin by taking it apart.

In the heart of the word is the root: MINISTER.

A *minister* is a servant, a helper of others, not one who receives service or help from them.

At the end is the common suffix: ATION.

The most common use of this suffix is to indicate an action or process. Thus, administration conveys the idea of doing ministry. Many people are reluctant to take an administrative role in the church because they feel it removes them from what they love doing most: ministry. Any job in the church that keeps someone from doing ministry should not be given the name administration.

At the front is the almost equally common prefix: AD.

This prefix means toward, or near, or alongside.

Therefore, the actual meaning of our English word, accurately reflecting the words used in the New Testament is as follows:

ADMINISTRATION = TO MINISTER ALONGSIDE

Ministering alongside others means working with people, sharing the load, encouraging, supporting, and enabling them to develop their gifts and potential. The effective administrator is part of a team of ministers who minister to other leaders as well as helping them minister to those for whom they are responsible.

In an educational ministry such as the Sunday school, the ultimate goal is to minister to the individual. The teacher or small group leader *ministers to* learners.

In order for teachers to be able to provide that ministry effectively, they need to experience the same type of ministry themselves. The teacher *ministers to* small group leaders. The department leader *ministers to* teachers.

Similarly, these leaders need to exper-ience ministry also. The division leader *ministers to* the department leader.

And of course, even division leaders need love and ministry support. The pastor *ministers to* division leaders.

Effective ministry is never a one-way street with one person having all the resources and energy and wisdom. So the whole process flows continually in both directions.

Ministry to someone who is also involved in ministry must always incorporate that person's ministry. In other words, the department leader's ministry to teachers includes working alongside them in their ministry to learners. Ministering alongside involves far more teaching by example than teaching by directive.

Complete the worksheet on page 125 to show the ministry responsibilities of those engaged in your church's educational ministries.

Structure: Horizontal and Vertical

In order for ministering alongside to occur throughout a church's educational

Pastor/Board			
Early Childhood Coordinator	**Children's Coordinator**	**Youth Coordinator**	**Adult Coordinator**
Program Leaders (Sunday school, Children's church, Weekday club, Children's choirs, VBS, etc.)	**Program Leaders** (Sunday school, Children's church, Weekday club, Children's choirs, VBS, etc.)	**Program Leaders** (Sunday school, youth groups, camps, etc.) Children's choirs,	**Program Leaders** (Sunday school, Home Bible studies, Men's /Women's ministries, etc.)
Department Leaders	**Department Leaders**	**Department Leaders**	**Department Leaders/ Teachers**
Teachers	**Teachers**	**Teachers**	**Teachers**

ministries, an effective organizational structure is needed that is clearly understood by everyone involved. This structure may be put together in one of two ways: by age level or by program agencies.

Horizontal: Age Level

This structural pattern links all ministries by age divisions. Thus, all early childhood programs are coordinated with a common leadership and philosophy. Meanwhile, all youth programs are similarly linked. While there must be some coordination between these age level endeavors, especially when they happen to meet at the same time (i.e., Sunday school) or share facilities, the major administrative structure works within each age division.

Many churches have a partial age-level structure. For example, a church with a part-time or full-time youth director will assign this person responsibility for all youth ministries. While some of these ministries may be part of a larger agency (i.e., Sunday school), there is usually more concern about the youth leader making the youth Sunday school classes link to the rest of the total youth program than to the rest of the Sunday school. As long as the teenagers start and end about the same time and do not excessively disturb other age levels, the leadership of the Sunday school tends to take a rather

"hands-off" approach and let the youth leaders "do their own thing."

Also, a degree of age-level structuring often happens informally when people accept more than one responsibility with an age group. Thus, a person who teaches a Sunday class and also works with the same age group in the weekday club or graded choir programs provides a significant link between the different programs.

Structuring a church's educational ministries by age levels has several advantages.

- Programs for people in each age level can be coordinated to provide comprehensive balance, avoiding excessive overlapping of content and activities, or omission of important areas.
- Leadership for each age level can focus on the unique needs and interests of that stage of life.
- A common philosophy of ministry can be implemented in all programs for a particular age level, producing a stronger cumulative impact in participants' lives than if each program operated on differing or conflicting sets of principles.
- Each program component can be effectively used to promote other programs for the same age level.
- Incorporation of new people benefits from easily shared information about visitors and attendance and from the

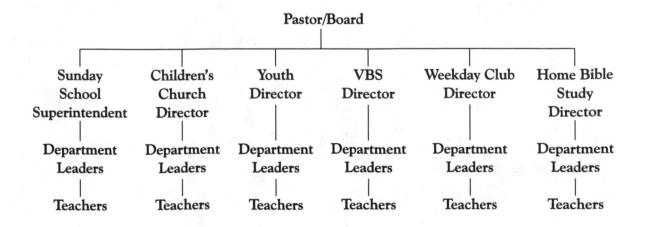

opportunities for learners to see some of the same leadership from one program to another.

- It is often easier to make major changes when a program is seen as part of the total ministry for an age level than when it is an independent entity.

Vertical: Program Agencies

The alternative to structuring by age levels is to structure by the various programs the church provides. Thus, the Sunday school, children's church, youth groups, age level choirs, home study groups, Vacation Bible School, camps, and so on are all separate organizations with their own leadership, structure, and philosophy.

Obviously, there are times when leaders of one program must interact with those in another one. And some people will serve in more than one program, providing an informal link between them.

Structuring a church's educational ministries by programs has several advantages.

- Each program can focus on its assigned distinctives. A particular program may involve significantly different activities and procedures from other programs for the same age level.
- Workers may have more in common with those working with other age levels in that same program than with people who work with the same age level in different programs.
- Program leaders have one program on which to focus. Age level leaders may not always be able to give adequate attention to all programs and some programs may get slighted.
- Some programs have helpful links to agencies outside the local church (denominational or club programs, etc.) that relate most efficiently to

the leadership of that specific program.

- Some programs simply work better in some churches if operated separately (but cooperatively) from other age level endeavors. For example, a program such as Vacation Bible School or camp that occurs only once a year may involve participants from more than one age level and be most efficiently run as a separate entity, rather than as part of the ongoing age level programs. On the other hand, if such programs operate independently, they may not succeed in guiding new people into the church's ongoing ministries.

As a church grows and adds part-time or full-time staff in administrative roles, gradually more of its educational ministries become organized by age levels. This shift from vertical to horizontal structure occurs in order to avoid having the church's growing ministries become fragmented or competitive.

Administrative Roles in the Sunday School

However a church chooses to organize itself for conducting its educational ministries, a variety of administrative roles must be shared among a leadership team. Forming a leadership team is not simply a matter of deciding what jobs need to be done and dividing them up among the available people. A leadership team is fully as much a ministry group as is a Sunday school class or home study group. The members of the leadership team must meet together often enough to be able to encourage and support each other, as well as to carry out their individual responsibilities.

The job descriptions on pages 127-134 are intended as guidelines to be adapted in planning and evaluating administrative functions. In each case, a very specific job description should be provided. If a job is worth asking someone to do, it is worth being defined in writing so that everyone involved clearly understands what each person has agreed to do. Job descriptions should be written and presented in terms of what actions will make the person successful in that ministry, not as statements of requirements by the program. People want to give their time to something of significance, so written job descriptions should define both the purpose of the position and the actions that will accomplish that purpose.

Length and Frequency of Service

"When I agreed to teach, I didn't know I would be receiving a life sentence in the three-year-olds' class," a teacher lamented.

Those who guide people in ministry must face the very practical matter of how long the person will be expected to engage in this ministry. Two major, somewhat contradictory principles, must be taken into account.

1. Ministry is a lifelong part of the Christian life. A Christian never moves beyond the privilege and responsibility of service. Plus, becoming skilled at a ministry usually requires that a person stay with it for a period of time.

2. People are reluctant to make long-term time and energy commitments, especially if they are uncertain about being capable of doing the task. People who have never been involved in a teaching or leadership position may find it difficult to envision themselves doing it at all,

let alone doing it for an extended time.

Provision must be made to encourage and nurture people in discovering the rich rewards of long-term, consistent ministry, while at the same time, finding ways to involve people for shorter periods of time. The challenge of involving busy people has led most churches to experiment with ways of adjusting the expected term of service for most ministry positions.

Open-End Commitment

Some churches enlist people for a teaching or leading position with the often unspoken understanding they will continue until they ask to be relieved or they are asked to step down. In many other situations, once a person has served well in an area, no one ever brings up the issue of how long that person will continue to serve, perhaps hoping that if the subject never comes up, the person will just keep right on and won't have to be replaced.

One advantage to open-end commitments is continuity. Another is that people become skilled at what they do.

A disadvantage of open-end commitments is that people may continue out of a sense of obligation ("Everybody expects me to do it.") rather than because of a fresh vision. Motivating or replacing a long-term "fixture" can be very difficult. New people observing such patterns may be even more reluctant to get involved fearing they will be expected to follow suit.

Multi-Year Commitment

Some administrative positions are deemed too essential to have frequent turnover, so churches enlist people for two or more years at a time. A person who serves adequately is often asked to continue beyond the initial commitment.

The obvious plus of such extended service is the continuity provided by people of experience.

Potential drawbacks to such arrangements include the following:

- People may begin to feel a program or position "belongs" to them.
- They may become unresponsive to changing needs.
- They may "burn out" after doing the same job for an extended period.
- It may become difficult to make a leadership change.
- Many people are reluctant to tackle a multi-year responsibility.

One approach that minimizes the drawbacks while retaining some of the advantages is having a new leader serve for a time, assisting an experienced leader. Then, after a stated time, the experienced leader takes a "sabbatical" or shifts to another responsibility; the new person assumes the leadership role.

One-Year Commitment

During most of the twentieth century, teachers in Sunday school and most other educational ministries typically served a year at a time. It was not at all uncommon for two-thirds to three-quarters of a teaching staff to recommit yearly to another year of service. Toward the end of the century, this pattern became far less common.

The one-year commitment has worked well for many people since it is long enough for most people to become fairly competent at the essential teaching and leading skills, and it allows opportunity to build relationships and see tangible growth in the lives of learners.

The one-year commitment intimidates many prospective teachers, and poses special problems during times of the year when people are likely to be out of town.

The School-Year Term

A variation of the one-year term is to have people serve for the nine or ten months of the school year. This works well in programs that do not function during the summer or when a separate staff can be enlisted to serve through those months.

The Semester Term

Some churches find it works well to enlist two sets of teachers and leaders, each of whom serves for half of the year. During the semester when teachers are not teaching, they serve as substitutes and prayer partners for those who are teaching.

July-January	Team A Teaches
	Team B Supports
February-June	Team A Supports
	Team B Teaches

This provides an ample pool of substitutes who are familiar with the learners and the teaching procedures. And the six-month term is long enough for relationships to be nourished and growth to occur.

Shorter Terms

Many programs enlist people for three months or less.

- **One quarter** (thirteen weeks)
- **One unit or month** (four to five weeks)

The shorter terms are effective ways to involve people who are reluctant or unable to commit to a longer period of service, while giving them a chance to use their gifts. Terms of one month usually allow teachers to complete a unit of lessons and to become acquainted with learners in the group. Many youth and adult groups like the shorter terms because they give the learners exposure to a variety of teachers over the course of a year.

Shorter terms may result in less-effective learning because they do not allow time for teachers to build in-depth relationships with learners. Shorter terms require more work by administrators to enlist, prepare, and support the additional people needed to staff the terms.

Rotating and Alternating Staffs

Many programs enlist people to serve once or twice a month, or even once a quarter. This is common in children's church and nursery programs, which many view simply as child care, and thus are programs that do not require continuity of personnel.

Since rotating positions tend to be the easiest level of responsibility, new people are more likely to agree to try them. Parents, especially, tend to be willing to take their turn.

However, rotating positions produce the least-satisfying results for a number of reasons.

- Teachers who are "taking turns" find it difficult to build relationships with learners they only see once a month or less.
- They are unlikely to engage in any out-of-class contacts with learners.
- They are more likely to view their upcoming "turn" with dread than people who have continuity with their group.
- They are less likely than continuing teachers to attend training sessions or to spend time preparing the session and improving their skills.

Administrative Functions

While a teacher's job is somewhat easy to define ("Just do what the teacher's manual says."), an administrator's job includes a wide variety of tasks and responsibilities. Administrators must take certain actions to lead an educational ministry effectively. A brief summary of these actions follows.

Planning and Calendaring

Someone has to look ahead. That someone had better be the administrator, looking beyond next Sunday, envisioning what changes and challenges, obstacles and opportunities might be faced.

Long Range: Goals and Objectives. The core of effective long-range planning is the process of setting goals and objectives and of defining strategies to meet those goals and objectives. Unless administrators are looking toward the future, a church's education program will find itself reacting to the unforeseen rather than taking the initiative to implement improvements.

Short Range: Events. "We're really disappointed in the turnout, but this was just not a good time to have [insert name of event that flopped]."

One of the immutable laws of church work is that there is *never* a good time to have an event. There will always be conflicts in people's schedules.

"Why is it the people who most need to be here are the ones least likely to attend?"

This frequently heard lament is often posed as though it were a comment on the weather, something to talk about but impossible to change.

Effective administrators recognize that the finest program possible is worthless to those who don't attend. Effective administrators consistently take a series of actions to secure the highest participation possible.

1. First, they plan their work. They start planning far in advance, and they schedule events at the least-inconvenient times possible. This requires coordination and cooperation among different groups in the church so that events involving the same people do not compete.

2. Second, they work their plan. They never assume that the people who need to attend an event will automatically show up. Effective leaders assume people have other things to do, so they conduct a thorough campaign to enlist participation. This includes the following:

Give ample advance notice. The larger the commitment being sought, the earlier people need to know.

Make many varied announcements. A single notice in the church bulletin will bring in the "faithful few" but is unlikely to get anyone else to attend. A combination of bulletin and newsletter notices, posters, postcards, and verbal announcements will make the average person aware that an important event is scheduled.

Make personal contacts. Everyone needs a person-to-person invitation and/or reminder, even those who know they ought to be at an event. Those who are considered the least likely to attend need extra contacts to enlist their participation.

Communicate the value of the event. Sadly, most people have experienced more than one meeting that was a total waste of their time. Why should teachers of adults be expected to sit through a discussion of discipline problems among the junior boys? Why should nursery workers be cajoled to attend a session on how to use flannelgraph? Why should parents of teenagers be drawn to a workshop that focuses on potty training and the tooth

fairy? Let people know what the event offers them and why it is important to them and to the church.

A vital tool for every administrator is a calendar that identifies the events of the next twelve months. More detailed planning can be done on a three-month calendar.

The sample planning calendars on pages 135 and 136 identify three types of events.

1. Training events are opportunities for teachers and leaders to improve their skills and expand their vision.

2. Outreach events are designed to attract new visitors, follow-up on visitors and absentees, and/or to add new groups that will better meet the needs of people you want to reach.

3. Special events are all new, periodic, or one-time events such as social activities, service projects, Sunday school promotions, teacher appreciation banquets, new courses, retreats, Vacation Bible School, and so on.

Recruiting

"I wouldn't mind being a leader if it weren't for having to recruit people. If I could ever get all my positions filled, then I could do my job."

This common complaint reflects honest feelings about the difficulty of recruiting. It also shows a significant misunderstanding of the administrative role. Chapter 7 gives specific help that will make the recruiting process both easier and more productive. At this point, we will briefly touch on the administrator's view of recruiting.

An administrator who wishes recruiting could be eliminated from his job is like a doctor who wishes to avoid treating sick people. He is like an evangelist who hopes no sinners will show up at a crusade. Every leader in a church's educational ministry must recognize that the process of encouraging people to get involved in ministry is a major part of the job. Administrators who are excited by a vision for teaching and reaching are the keys to building a team of teachers and leaders who will make a positive difference in the life and ministry of the church. Far from being a task that keeps a leader from doing the "real" work of administration, recruiting is at the very heart of what an administrator's mission involves.

Identify Needs. It doesn't take great insight to realize that a problem exists when the third-grade boys do not have a teacher for their class. However, far too many administrators limit their recruiting to "filling holes" by finding someone who is willing to step into a vacancy. Instead, administrators must be looking ahead, anticipating when growth, promotion, and changes in people's lives will require additional staff.

Build a Climate. The manner in which administrators recruit staff sets a tone for educational ministries, both among those who agree to serve and those who decline. If contacting people about getting involved is seen as an unpleasant chore, then others will quickly perceive ministry as sentences to endure rather than opportunities to serve and grow. The administrator who shames or cajoles people into "doing their duty" will find it difficult, if not impossible, ever to motivate those people to be enthusiastic about ministry.

Equip and Nurture Personnel

Once a person has agreed to serve, the administrator's responsibility has not ended. Leaders who enlist people for ministry have a great obligation and privilege to support those people so that they succeed at their assignments. Unfortunately, far too many churches give people jobs to do, then leave them on their own, causing them to flounder.

(See Chapter 7 for information on how to guide a new person's development so they become effective in ministry.)

Manage Operations

Administrators are responsible to guide all the activity within their department, division, or program area. This does not mean the administrator must be a one-man band or one-woman show. It simply means the administrator must work alongside, supporting, encouraging, and advising those who are a part of that leader's ministry team. Effective management involves these important factors.

Create Structure. The leader is responsible to organize so that each person involved is able to serve effectively. This includes setting clear expectations of what each person is to do, assigning each person enough responsibility to challenge him/her, while staying well within each person's limits of time, energy, and skill.

For example, a new teacher usually needs to hear the department leader say, "I'd like you to lead this activity, since it's fairly simple and will let you focus on getting to know the students." Such thoughtful guidance is preferable to asking, "Why don't you read these eight pages and let me know which activity you'd prefer to lead?"

Focus on Priorities. Leaders are responsible to make sure ministry team members know the objectives for their area and how these goals fit into the overall objectives of the church. Then, as the team works together, the leader is responsible to keep the group's efforts moving toward those goals. As much as possible, the leader should encourage team members to suggest ideas for reaching the goals and for modifying them to fit their specific area of ministry better.

Coordinate and Communicate. In our busy, often hectic society, getting two or more people working together is no easy achievement. Yet that is what a leader must do. Even though each person on a ministry team understands his/her function and is aware of the program's priorities, this is no guarantee that the ministry will be carried out effectively. Administrators must talk regularly to everyone involved, checking on progress, making sure that what Mary intends to do does not get in the way of John's assignment. Administrators must make sure that the team's great ideas do not "fall through the cracks" because no one specifically agreed to do them.

Control the Range of Relationships. Several times, this manual has made the point that a leader can support and encourage only five to eight people on a ministry team. Even Jesus, the Master Teacher, limited his "ministry team" to twelve, and they basically lived with him for three years. This ensured that each one received ample personal attention. In a volunteer program where people see each other for a limited time only once or twice a week, few administrators have the time or the skill to directly guide more than five to eight people. Thus, the department leader in the following example is nearing the maximum number of teachers he/she can effectively lead.

DEPARTMENT LEADER

Teacher Teacher Teacher Teacher Teacher

When another teacher is added to this staff, a new department should be started.

Similarly, this division coordinator is nearing the maximum number of departments he/she can effectively lead, especially if the coordinator is a volunteer. A coordinator who is hired either part time or full time may be able to guide several more departments, provided numerous other responsibilities (clerical, custodial, etc.) are not added to the job description.

DIVISION COORDINATOR

Dept. Leader   Dept. Leader   Dept. Leader   Dept. Leader   Dept. Leader

When another department is added to this division, a new division should be started.

Multiply Yourself. Just as a basketball coach is not measured by how well he/she shoots or dribbles but by how well the players perform, an administrator is not measured by his/her own skill but by the ministry done by others. Unfortunately, too many leaders take the short cut of doing too many things themselves. ("I just don't have time to get someone else to do this." "It's so much easier to do it myself." "The only way to make sure it's done right is for me to do it."). Besides abrogating the basic principle of administration (minister alongside), this limits the accomplishments to what one person can do. By engaging just one other person to share the task, ultimately twice as much can be achieved.

The ultimate measure of any administrator is taken once that person is no longer involved. The effective leader looks to the future, preparing people to continue and expand the ministry even if the leader is no longer on the scene. It is not a compliment to say of a former leader, "Things have never gone as well since he/she left."

Be very cautious about a new leader who subscribes to the "honeymoon" theory of leadership: "I've got to make as many changes as possible before people stop going along just to be polite." The urge to "make my own mark" coupled with a belief that "anything my predecessor did can't be very good" does not build on the foundations laid by previous generations of leaders. Instead, it causes churches to lurch along ineffectively.

The effective administrator realizes that programs are transitory, but people live a lifetime. By focusing on building lives rather than programs, a leader's time and energy will produce results that truly last.

Lead Meetings

"Not another meeting! I sure hope they've found a way to run heaven without meetings!" What administrator has not groaned at the prospect of another meeting?

Most of us oppose meetings because we have attended (and/or led) so many that were uninteresting and unproductive. A well-run meeting that gets things done generates excitement and satisfaction, even for those who are bone weary from a long day.

While each person who attends a meeting contributes to its success or failure, the person who leads the meeting has the key responsibility. Even when a meeting involves only two people, one person must guide the process toward its intended purpose. Administrators in educational ministries will lead two major kinds of meetings: business meetings and training, motivational meetings.

Business Meetings. Administrators must lead business meetings, otherwise known as board or committee meetings. If a program is active, people will need to get together to make some group decisions. The following guidelines are useful when planning and conducting meetings of this type:

1. *Train group members to submit agenda items in advance.* They should also clearly define alternative courses of action. Members must avoid bringing up items they have not clearly thought through. Vague issues waste everyone's time. (e.g., "I've been thinking it would be nice to do something different for Promotion Sunday. Does anyone have any ideas?")

2. *Make an agenda.* Plan ahead the specific items to be discussed and the order in which they will be considered. Set a suggested time schedule as a guide, indicating which items might need more time than others. Whenever possible, spell out the specific action or alternatives being recommended. A sample agenda is on page 137.

3. *Reserve time for prayer and sharing.* Before addressing the business at hand, plan a time for leading the group in praying for one another's personal and ministry needs and victories. Team members need to take time to build relationships and nurture spiritual vitality.

4. *Focus on the future.* Many church boards and committees spend more time looking at what has already happened than in planning what needs to happen. While a measure of time should be given to reporting and evaluating completed activities, reserve the majority of the time for upcoming events.

5. *Emphasize items that involve everyone.* While it may be necessary to discuss certain matters that directly impact only one person or group, prevent such business from absorbing the meeting time. One way to do this is to refer such items to a

subgroup that will make a recommendation or a decision. Another approach is to develop guidelines for items that do not require a group decision. For example, give each person or group a discretionary budget that can be spent for ministry purposes without prior approval of the group.

6. *Distribute the agenda in advance.* Give participants advance notice of what will be done in the meeting.

7. *Keep the meeting on track.* If someone raises an item not on the agenda, lead the group to decide whether to refer to the next meeting or deal with it now. If the latter, the group needs to realize that some other item may need to be deferred.

8. *Seek maximum participation.* Ask those who have not said much to share their thoughts. Ask those who have spoken a lot to defer to someone who has not yet spoken.

9. *Strive for consensus.* Building a team is more important than any specific agenda item. When strong disagreement on a proposal exists, ask questions to help bring people together.

- "How much of what (Bill) said do you agree with?"
- "What is your understanding of why (Christ) prefers the other plan?"
- "What approach could satisfy the concerns on both sides?"

10. *Affirm people for their ideas.* You need not agree with a comment to thank a person for sharing his/her thoughts.

11. *Clearly define the actions to be taken as a result of the meeting.* Do this as a summary at the end of the meeting and in a written report. Send the report to each team member as soon as possible after the meeting.

Training and Motivational Meetings. Administrators must also lead meetings that train and motivate teachers and leaders. To make these sessions productive, administrators must be skilled at these functions.

1. *Emphasize personal contact in promotional efforts.* Personally tell people why their attendance at the meeting is important.

2. *Provide fellowship and inspiration.* While skill development is very important, it is even more vital that volunteers develop a sense of belonging. A shared purpose motivates people to do their best.

3. *Present a balance of "how to" and "here's why."* People not only need to learn how to do ministry, they need to know why those actions are valuable. Make sure the skills being taught are appropriate to use with the age groups taught by those attending the meeting.

4. *Demonstrate the skills teachers and leaders need to use in their ministries.* Because people tend to teach the way they were taught, a lecture on creative ways to involve people in active learning will have very little impact. The examples people see demonstrated are the ones they will try.

5. *Give hands-on experience with the skills being taught.* Once people have seen a skill demonstrated, they need a safe opportunity to practice it. If the skill is teaching people to use music as a learning experience in their classrooms, let them practice learning and singing songs they will use.

6. *Link the skills being taught to the lessons participants will teach next.* It does little good to train people to use a particular teaching skill without showing where to use the skills in a real class session.

(*Chapter 7 presents information on the components of effective training.*)

Use Resources

Administrators are responsible for making effective use of the resources allotted to their area of ministry and for communicating resource needs to responsible individuals or groups.

Time. The most fleeting of the resources at our disposal, time is perhaps the most difficult of all to manage effectively. Using time wisely is of paramount importance, especially in programs that meet only once a week, or less, and that involve volunteers whose available time is limited. In every type of ministry, there is always more work to do than time in which to do it. As one leader put it, "It's not the things I do that wear me down, it's the things I can't get to."

The Administrator's Time: An administrator must be a good steward of his/her own time. This requires setting priorities, so that the available time is spent on that which is most important, or in many cases, that which is most likely to produce results. It is usually not too difficult to fit in the scheduled events and meetings, although it can be a challenge. The hard part is blocking out time in which to work on all the behind-the-scenes things that need to be done, but do not have a specific time slot attached to them. For example, when will an administrator find time to:

- Check in with a team member who has been facing problems at work or at home?
- Start making those recruiting phone calls that don't need to be completed for several months?
- Talk individually with team members about their ongoing responsibilities or their attendance at an upcoming event or meeting?
- Read books and magazines related to his/her ministry?

A busy person will never "find" time for all that needs to be done. The only solution is to "make" time. There are several ways to take control of time so that it is used as productively as possible.

1. Set aside the same time period every week for doing administrative tasks. Block this time period on your calendar well in advance so that other activities are not allowed to intrude. If your schedule is not regular enough to allow the same time block to be protected every week, set aside a specific time period within each week. Work on your calendar at least a month in advance to block out time in every week.

2. Make a weekly "to do" list of the tasks needing to be done that week. Mark each item to indicate its relative importance (i.e., A, B, C). See the "Eight-Day Weekly Planner" on page 138.

3. Schedule one or more team members to work with you. For example, if you have twenty phone calls to make, arrange to meet one or more team members at the church office. If the church has more than one phone line, divide the calls among you. Stop once or twice to compare notes on the responses you are getting. If the church has only one phone line, alternate making the calls. Make sure you are involving team members to work with you on tasks that fit in their job description.

4. Start with the most important items on the "to do" list. (It's no crime to slip in a few lesser items that can be handled quickly in order to give yourself the satisfaction of marking something on the list as being completed.)

The Team Members' Time: Follow the same pattern as above in helping other team members use their time wisely. A department leader needs to help teachers schedule time for lesson planning and outreach efforts. A division coordinator needs to help department leaders develop effective training and growth experiences for teachers.

Finances. Money is perhaps the most sensitive resource—both the money that is received as income (offerings, fees, etc.) and the money that is allocated for expenses.

Some churches expect their educational ministries to fund their own costs of operation (usually not including building costs). For example, the Sunday school offering is retained by the Sunday school leadership for purchasing curriculum and supplies.

Other churches see their educational ministries as agencies of the total church that are funded by the total congregation. These churches combine any income from educational ministries into the general fund, then pay the expenses for those ministries, usually without any attempt to compare a group's income with its expense. Often, any offerings received or fees charged are seen primarily as means to help children and young people learn to be good stewards.

In either case, camps, retreats, and other special events are commonly paid for through the fees (and a few scholarships) charged to those who attend.

Curriculum. Curriculum resources are key components in determining and implementing the church's teaching and learning objectives for each age level. A church that declares that life application of Scripture is a major goal would be foolish to adopt a curriculum that emphasizes content with little or no attention given to application. Similarly, it makes little sense for a church to say that it wants to actively involve learners in using the Bible themselves, and then select a curriculum that rarely if ever guides the teacher to have learners open the Bible in class. Or, why would a church buy curriculum designed for a particular approach to teaching, then leave teachers to adapt it extensively to fit their individual preferences?

Unfortunately, while churches spend a significant amount of money on curriculum, few give even a little attention to ensuring that their teachers know how to use it effectively. Typically, a few weeks before the start of a new quarter, curriculum is distributed to the teaching staff along with an unspoken message: "Hope you know what to do with all this stuff!" It is also common for experienced teachers and leaders to adapt the curriculum so much that new teachers see little connection between the curriculum and what actually happens in a class. Training sessions tend to deal with skills and procedures that do not appear in the curriculum from week to week. Often administrators spend more time figuring out how many pieces to order than planning ways to ensure teachers make effective use of their resources. The result is that new teachers find it much more difficult than necessary to get started, and experienced teachers reinforce teaching procedures that are familiar, rather than letting their curriculum stretch them to try a wider variety of approaches.

The curriculum materials your church uses are a remarkable resource, too valuable to misuse. The checklist on page 126 will help you tap their full potential.

Equipment and Supplies. Administrators are also responsible for managing equipment and supplies. (*This aspect of administration is dealt with in Chapter 8.*)

Deal With Problems and Special Situations

One aspect of administration that keeps life interesting, and sometimes frustrating, is that unforeseen challenges always pop up. No matter how meticulously a church plans, something will occur that was not expected. No matter how well the organizational structure is designed, a church is bound to find that someone does not seem to fit in the groups it has provided. We usually call these unexpected challenges "problems." The effective administrator learns to approach them as "opportunities." Changing one's perspective on facing administrative challenges is not merely an exercise in positive thinking, although that has real value. Viewing problems as opportunities gets to the core of why good administration is so vital in the life of a church.

"I'd love working in a growing church if it just weren't for all the added people I have to deal with." This tongue-in-cheek complaint recognizes that the most important issues in administration are people issues. People take precedence over programs. Thus, a problem always contains within it the potential to benefit people in some manner. Rather than keeping us from ministry, problems direct our ministry to particular areas of need.

Child Safety. Protecting children and those who work with children is one of the most sensitive and difficult matters facing church leaders. The church is not exempt from the plague of child abuse that haunts our society. Carefully defined policies and procedures are needed to keep a church as safe a haven as possible. Policies need to be developed and consistently implemented in these areas.

1. *Selecting Staff for Children and Youth*

All who serve in areas involving children and young people will complete an information form that includes how long the person has been active in the congregation, any other churches in which he/she has been involved in recent years, whether or not the person has ever been convicted or pleaded guilty to child abuse or a crime involving actual or attempted sexual molestation of a minor. (*See sample information form in Chapter 7.*)

Responsible individuals or group designated by the church will conduct a personal interview with the volunteer candidate before he/she is appointed.

A responsible person will check the personal references given by the prospective teacher or leader.

A minimum time period and level of involvement in the congregation (i.e., an active member for at least six months) should be required before a person is allowed to work in ministries with children and youth.

2. *Guiding Staff for Children and Youth*

Conduct training sessions for staff that include a clear explanation of the church's policies and procedures.

Require that all children's groups have at least two workers present at all times.

Have at least one administrative person visibly circulating among all groups. Whenever possible, groups should meet in rooms with open doors and window blinds.

Require that all one-to-one ministry be carried out by an adult of the same gender in a public area visible to others.

Establish a minimum and maximum age (i.e., 25 and 65 years) for drivers providing transportation for church-sponsored events. Also require that a driver form be completed in advance with information on the person's driving record, the vehicle, and the insurance. The completed form should be approved by a responsible person who is knowledgeable about the church's insurance coverage and any applicable restrictions.

Clearly define the procedures recommended for dealing with discipline problems at each age level. Provide training sessions in utilizing these approaches.

Sample guidelines for children's safety are on page 139.

Behavior Problems. The presence of children and teenagers virtually guarantees that some behavior problems will occur. Dealing with unacceptable behaviors can be a challenging problem. First, workers in once-a-week programs often start over every week in dealing with recurring problem behaviors. Most congregations, especially those with a variety of adult leaders and volunteers, have differing opinions about how to respond when misbehavior occurs. One problem this creates is that many youngsters learn more about how much they can get away with when Mrs. Jones is teaching than they do about worship or the Bible.

In programs where God's love is being proclaimed, the manner in which unlovable behaviors and attitudes are handled is as important as the words teachers say. Therefore, a few clearly defined guidelines can aid workers in being prepared to deal with problems effectively and consistently.

Sample guidelines for discipline are on page 140.

Persons With Disabilities. One important change in our society and in churches over the past generation has been a growing awareness of the rights and needs of people with disabilities. The most visible signs of this awareness are the signs on parking spaces, wheelchair ramps, and rest room doors. Beyond those external evidences, churches in ever-growing numbers are responding by sharing God's love with all people, including those facing physical, mental, and emotional challenges.

Typically, churches have not addressed the needs of persons with disabilities until they encountered a specific situation. Most commonly, changes occurred when a building permit required a church either to modify or build features to provide access to the church's facilities.

Often ministries to disabled persons began with the concern of just one friend or relative. Their child had Down syndrome. Their student was in a wheelchair. Their neighbor was deaf. They started a program to help this person, and a whole ministry to disabled persons grew out of it.

Sometimes churches recognized the need to minister to people with disabilities only when such a person arrived in their midst. Usually, a measure of frantic conferring took place in an attempt to decide what to do with this person who did not fit into the church's expected pattern of ministry. Unfortunately, such discussions sometimes took on the tone of dealing with a nuisance, rather than seeing an opportunity to minister in Christian love.

Gradually, over the years, those perceptions have given way to effective, coordinated efforts to fully include people with disabilities in the life of God's people. Churches have learned that the great majority of people with disabilities, even most of those with mental retardation, can respond to the good news of God's love. The growth of such ministries has also uncovered rich opportunities for outreach, as churches have found family members of the disabled tend to be very receptive to churches that demonstrate genuine caring.

Just a few years ago, the two most common patterns of ministry to people with disabilities were either to place them in special groups or classes or to keep them at home with a family member or caregiver. Gradually, church leaders and volunteers have come to realize that for a large number of such people, it is better for them and for the church to include them in regular groups. Also, parents have become accustomed to their children and teens with special needs being "mainstreamed" into regular classes in public school. This experience has produced a whole generation of advocates for similar treatment in church programs.

The brief guidelines on page 141 are useful in starting to build an effective ministry with persons who have disabilities and their families.

Persons With AIDS. A related challenge for churches involves developing policies for ministering to persons with HIV infection or AIDS. (Human immunodeficiency virus, HIV, kills white blood cells, ultimately destroying the body's ability to fight off infections. As the disease progresses, relatively harmless germs cause life-threatening disease and the person is said to have AIDS, acquired immunodeficiency syndrome.) Many congregations have sought to minister both spiritually and physically to those affected.

Sadly, effective ministry to persons with HIV infections is often hampered by fear of contagion. Since HIV virus is spread from person to person by either sexual intercourse or blood contact, people need not fear exposure through casual contacts with a person who has been infected.

As with ministry to persons with disabilities, most churches tend to address this matter only when they directly encounter the problem. Unfortunately, waiting to develop thoughtful, compassionate policies until faced with an infected person leaves the church vulnerable to strong, and often conflicting, emotions. Without clearly defined policies in place before the need arises, the people who most need to be helped and supported by the church may instead be deeply hurt by uncertainty, misinformation, and even hysterical response.

Four major areas need to be considered:

1. *Education* for leaders, teachers, and members, as well as for the person with HIV infection and his/her family.

The congregation needs to be informed about AIDS, the ways in which it can and cannot be spread, responsible actions to contain its spread, and ways to minister to those in need. Unless such information is provided, people are unlikely to support efforts to accept and include persons with HIV infection or AIDS.

Persons who are infected, and their families, need the same information in order to help alleviate the fears of others so that supportive ministry can be provided.

2. *Confidentiality,* balancing the common desire for privacy on the part of a person infected by HIV, and the right of others to know of any potential risks.

Until the congregation has been effectively informed about HIV infections and AIDS, fear will keep those who are infected from making their situation known. Fear will also keep those who are not infected from reaching out to someone in need.

3. *Support,* providing practical assistance to the person with HIV infection and his/her family.

Depending on the stage of the disease, the church may see the need to help with child care, household chores, transportation, food preparation, shopping, companionship, etc.

4. *Involvement,* finding ways to responsibly enable the person with HIV infection to participate as fully as possible in the life of the church.

Any fear or misunderstanding that may arise in ministering to persons with HIV infection is likely to focus in this area. However, if the educational efforts are effectively carried out, most people will accept the reasonable precautions needed to prevent the spread, not only of HIV infection, but of other contagious diseases, also.

The brief guidelines on page 142 are useful in starting to build an effective ministry with persons who have HIV infection and with their families.

Administration =
To Minister Alongside

In an educational ministry such as the Sunday school, the ultimate goal is to minister to the individual.

Teacher or small group leader   *ministers to*   learners.

In order for teachers to be able to provide that ministry effectively, they need to experience the same type of ministry themselves.

Teacher   *ministers to*   small group leaders.

Department leader   *ministers to*   teachers.

Similarly, these leaders need to experience ministry also.

Division leader   *ministers to*   department leader.

And of course, even division leaders need love and ministry support.

Pastor   *ministers to*   division leaders.

Effective ministry is never a one-way street with one person having all the resources and energy and wisdom. So the whole process flows continually in both directions.

Ministry to someone who is also involved in ministry must always incorporate that person's ministry. In other words, the department leader's ministry to teachers includes working alongside them in their ministry to learners. Ministering alongside involves far more teaching by example than teaching by directive.

Complete a chart showing the ministry responsibilities of those engaged in your church's educational ministries.

Administration = to Minister Alongside

_____   ministers to   _____

_____   ministers to   _____

_____   ministers to   _____

_____   ministers to   _____

_____   ministers to   _____

_____   ministers to   _____

_____   ministers to   _____

_____   ministers to   _____

Using Curriculum

Mark the actions to rate your present and planned curriculum use.

E=Excellent
S=Satisfactorily Doing Now
I=Improvement Needed
N=Need to Start

Curriculum Checklist

Item	Action	Comment

_____ 1. Curriculum is selected to reflect and help us achieve our stated ministry objectives.

_____ Early Childhood

_____ Children

_____ Youth

_____ Adult

_____ 2. Curriculum is selected with similar session formats throughout all groups within an age division, allowing all staff within the division to share similar understandings of teaching procedures.

_____ 3. Every new teacher is given a personal "walk-through" of current curriculum resources, with explanations of how it is used to help achieve ministry objectives.

_____ 4. Observation opportunities are provided for new and experienced teachers in which curriculum is demonstrated with no more than minimal adaptation.

_____ 5. Training sessions focus on using procedures and skills that are regularly suggested in the curriculum.

_____ 6. _____

_____

_____

JOB DESCRIPTION
The Leadership Team
(Christian Education Committee)

Basic Role

The leadership team may include the board or committee responsible for over-
sight of educational ministries and/or the key leaders of those ministries.
As a team, they are responsible for the overall direction, planning, and
operation of the church's ministries that focus on reaching people for
Christ and teaching them to grow in all areas of their Christian lives.
Other leadership teams may be established within specific age divisions
(e.g., children) or programs (e.g., Sunday school).

Major Functions

- Set goals and priorities that complement the overall church objectives.
- Identify major ways in which the goals will be achieved.
  - √ Develop plans for reaching new people (Chapter 2).
  - √ Define the teaching/learning plan and policies to be followed (Chapters 3 and 4).
  - √ Identify the staffing needed to implement that plan and the strategy for enlisting and training personnel (Chapter 7).
  - √ Project the facilities, equipment, resources needed (Chapter 8).
- Set dates on a calendar for major events that impact educational min-
  istries.
- Communicate goals and the plans for action to the staff, other church
  leaders, and the congregation.
- Evaluate progress toward those goals.

The Shepherd: Pastor/Minister

Basic Role

The senior pastor (or in cooperation with one or more members of the pastoral staff) is responsible for the overall direction of the church's educational ministry. The pastor works with the leadership team to set goals and evaluate progress in reaching people for Christ and in guiding their growth in the Christian life.

Major Functions

- Provide counsel and assistance in enlisting and preparing the other members of the leadership team.

- Guide the team in maintaining their focus on the ministry objectives.

- Give public support and recognition for the educational ministries and those involved in them.

- Assist other leaders as needed in fulfilling their ministry responsibilities.

The Specialists:
Age Level and
Program Directors

Basic Role

Whether full-time, part-time, or volunteer, the leaders who guide the major educational program efforts are vital to their success. Whether coordinating the ministries for a particular age division or directing a specific program (i.e., Sunday school), each leader is responsible for planning, organizing, staffing, leading, and evaluating an area of ministry to see that the stated ministry objectives are being achieved in reaching people for Christ and nurturing their growth in the Christian life.

Note: In order for an educational ministry to grow, adequate administrative support is necessary. If a leader is directly responsible for more than five to eight people, some of those people will receive only minimal attention from their leader. Thus, additional leaders must be developed to assume responsibility for a defined area within the program. See discussion on "Range of Relationships" in the "Manage Operations" section of this chapter.

Major Functions

- Meet regularly with the leadership team.
- Communicate goals and strategies to staff and participants and evaluate progress toward those goals.
- Lead staff in developing and implementing appropriate teaching plans and organizational structures.
- Direct efforts to identify, enlist, and train new staff (Chapter 7).
- Regularly observe teachers and leaders in action, offering encouragement, affirmation, and direction (Chapter 3).
- Lead staff in evaluating facility, resource, and curriculum needs and recommend actions to maintain and improve these items (Chapter 8).

Outreach Director

Basic Role

The outreach director is a specialized leader who has a deep concern for those who need to be reached. This person should be part of the leadership team and is responsible to see that the goal of reaching new people remains a top priority in everything done through educational programs.

Major Functions

- Meet regularly with the leadership team.
- Enlist an outreach leader for each program or department to work with those staff members in their outreach efforts.
- Promote outreach objectives with all staff members.
- Encourage and assist staff members in outreach efforts (visitor follow-up, encouraging members to invite unchurched friends, planning events with appeal to the unchurched, etc.).
- Ensure that accurate records are kept so that contacts with visitors and prospects can be effectively maintained.
- Cooperate with the church's evangelism and outreach efforts to build bridges for people reached through those endeavors.

JOB DESCRIPTION
The Support Staff (Office, Custodial, Library)

Basic Role

One does not have to be around a church long to realize the vital importance of the support staff. While these people may never be seen by the public and are rarely given the recognition they deserve, they are often the difference between a program's success or failure. The failure side tends to occur most often when support staff are uninformed and are thus unable to provide the quality of help needed. A wise administrator sets a high priority on building good working relationships with support staff, enlisting their commitment to the goals of reaching and teaching, and then keeping them informed—well in advance—of actions being taken and events being planned to reach those goals.

Major Functions

- Bailing out preoccupied administrators who forget crucial details in planning activities.

- Doing whatever needs to be done in a great deal less time than it ordinarily takes to do.

- Cheerfully enduring repeated interruptions from church members, the pastor, committee representatives, the pastor's wife, church officers, the pastor's children, and so on while still managing to do whatever needs to be done.

- It also helps if support staff can leap tall buildings at a single bound.

The support staff usually are not employed by the educational ministries and tend to be responsible to someone other than the educational administrators.

JOB DESCRIPTION
The Select: Volunteer Leaders and Teachers

Basic Role

The majority of people who volunteer in a church's educational ministries fit into three major categories:

- Division coordinators, department leaders, and others who take on administrative functions, seeking to encourage and support teachers in their ministry efforts;
- Teachers and group leaders who guide learners in study, fellowship, service, and outreach;
- Aides, helpers, and substitutes who want to be involved on a limited basis.

Major Functions

Division coordinators are responsible to their age level or program directors for the total ministry of their division, which includes planning, organizing, staffing, leading, and evaluating efforts to reach people and guide their continued growth in the Christian life. Coordinators must work closely with department leaders, encouraging, observing, and assisting in their tasks.

- Guide the divisional staff in identifying staffing needs; enlist and train new staff (Chapter 7).
- Regularly observe leaders and teachers in action, offering encouragement, affirmation, and direction (Chapter 3).
- Meet regularly with department leaders for planning and evaluation.
- Evaluate facility and resource needs and recommend actions to maintain and improve these items (Chapter 8).

Department leaders are responsible to their division coordinator or program director for the total ministry of their department, which includes guiding the staff in reaching people for Christ and guiding their growth in Christian life. Department leaders must work closely with teachers, encouraging, observing, and assisting in their tasks.

- Meet with teachers for prayer and sharing and to exchange ideas, plan sessions, make assignments, and select supplies.
- Early Childhood/Children/Youth—Welcome learners as they arrive, guiding them to get involved with activities teachers have prepared and/or to get to know others in the group.

- Early Childhood/Children/Youth—Assist teachers as needed in guiding the learning experiences, alerting teachers when it is time to move on to the next activity.
- Early Childhood/Children/Youth—Lead the parts of the session that involve all learners and teachers together.
- Observe teachers in action, offering encouragement, affirmation, and direction (Chapter 3).
- Evaluate facility and resource needs and recommend actions to maintain and improve these items (Chapter 8).

While teachers, group leaders, aides, and others are not administrative positions, those who are administrators need to know what these roles entail so they can assist these people in successfully fulfilling their ministry functions.

A *teaching team* is two or more people (leader, teachers, aides, etc.) working together to teach the same lesson to learners in the same room or rooms. Team teaching may take many different forms as people work out their mutual responsibilities. People who merely take turns teaching are not really working together as a team; they are simply substituting for each other.

Teachers are responsible for reaching people for Christ and for guiding their growth in the Christian life. In fulfilling this mission, teachers must plan contacts with learners both away from class and in the class sessions. They must set up a positive learning situation, then guide and involve learners in active exploration and application of Bible content.

- Be an example to learners of Christ's love, demonstrating growth in the qualities being taught.
- Select appropriate learning activities for each session.
- Guide learners in active learning experiences that contribute to understanding and application of Bible truth.
- Build a personal, caring relationship with each learner, both during the class and during the week;
- Seek to win unchurched individuals and families to Christ and to help them get involved in the life of the church.

Group Leaders (adult classes) serve as directed by the teacher. They seek to nurture a caring relationship with those assigned to their small group in order to reach people for Christ and aid their growth in the Christian life:

- Contact group members during the week to build supportive, caring friendship.
- Welcome group members when they attend class.
- During class sessions, when instructed by the teacher, guide small group learning experiences (may or may not involve members of assigned group).
- Organize periodic fellowship, study, and support meetings of those in their small group.

JOB DESCRIPTION:
The Select: Volunteer Leaders and Teachers
2

Aides, Helpers, and Substitutes assist teachers as needed. They may include:

- Potential teachers or group leaders who are not yet ready to make the commitment to accept a teacher position;
- People whose schedules, family situations, or health do not allow them to fulfill the responsibilities of a teacher, but who have useful gifts and abilities and should be provided opportunities to contribute;
- Teenagers who want to be involved in ministry and need opportunities to do so with the close supervision and guidance of an experienced teacher.

Specific assignments may depend as much on the person's availability, experience, maturity, and commitment as on the needs of the department or class in which he/she serves. Regardless of how brief or limited a person's service may be, a specific written statement is needed of what each person is to do and what that person's effort will accomplish.

JOB DESCRIPTION
The Saints: Congregation

Basic Role

The people who attend the classes and groups are not just the intended recipients of all the good that the leaders and teachers have planned. The objective of the educational ministries is not just to strengthen the learners, but "to prepare God's people for works of service, so that the body of Christ may be built up" (Ephesians 4:12).

Major Functions

- The congregation is not the audience for whom teachers perform. The congregation is the work force that receives guidance, encouragement, and occasionally correction, from the teachers the church has appointed.
- The congregation is also the source for leaders and teachers. The objective (especially in adult groups) must not be to measure success by how many people are sitting and listening, but by how many people have been prepared and enlisted in active service.
- The congregation is also the link to those needing to be reached. The members of the congregation are the ones who know individuals and families in the community who need the message and ministry of the church.

Twelve-Month Planning Calendar

Training events are opportunities for teachers and leaders to improve their skills and expand their vision.

Outreach events are designed to attract new visitors, follow-up on visitors and absentees, and/or to add new groups that will better meet the needs of people you want to reach.

Special events are all new, periodic, or one-time events such as social activities, service projects, Sunday school promotions, teacher appreciation banquets, new courses, retreats, Vacation Bible School, and so on.

**Twelve-Month
Planning Calendar**

Month: _____	Month: _____	Month: _____
Training	Training	Training
Outreach	Outreach	Outreach
Special	Special	Special
Month: _____	**Month:** _____	**Month:** _____
Training	Training	Training
Outreach	Outreach	Outreach
Special	Special	Special
Month: _____	**Month:** _____	**Month:** _____
Training	Training	Training
Outreach	Outreach	Outreach
Special	Special	Special
Month: _____	**Month:** _____	**Month:** _____
Training	Training	Training
Outreach	Outreach	Outreach
Special	Special	Special

Three-Month Planning Calendar

Training events are opportunities for teachers and leaders to improve their skills and expand their vision.

Outreach events are designed to attract new visitors, follow-up on visitors and absentees, and/or to add new groups that will better meet the needs of people you want to reach.

Special events are all new, periodic, or one-time events such as social activities, service projects, Sunday school promotions, teacher appreciation banquets, new courses, retreats, Vacation Bible School, and so on.

Three-Month Planning Calendar

Month: _____	Month: _____	Month: _____
Training	Training	Training
Outreach	Outreach	Outreach
Special	Special	Special

Sample Agenda

The time allotments shown accommodate a sixty- to ninety-minute meeting.

Time	Topic	Actions/Notes
10-20 min.	Prayer/Sharing	Personal/Ministry Praise Reports
		Personal/Ministry Needs
10-20 min.	Reports	Finances
		Projects Completed
		Projects in Process
40-50 min.	Planning	Curriculum
		Outreach
		Training
		Special/Other
Adjourn		

Eight-Day Weekly Planner

Things To Do	Date: This Week's Schedule
_____	Sunday
_____	
_____	
_____	Monday
_____	
_____	
_____	Tuesday
_____	
People to See/Meetings	Wednesday
_____	
_____	
_____	Thursday
_____	
People to Call	Friday
_____	
_____	
_____	Saturday
_____	
_____	Sunday
_____	
_____	

Sample Guidelines for Children's Safety

All workers and volunteers in children's programs are part of a ministry team guided by designated children's ministry leaders. Everyone involved in children's programs must comply with these policies to ensure a safe and secure environment for children and staff.

1. Each group of children shall have a minimum of two responsible workers, at least one being an adult, present at all times.

2. For children up through kindergarten age, at least one worker will be enlisted for every five (5) children. With elementary aged children, at least one worker for every eight (8) children will be provided.

3. One or more supervisors will circulate among rooms whenever children's activities are being held. Parents and other approved observers are welcome to visit children's programs at any time. Window blinds and doors are to be kept open whenever possible.

4. When taking children to the rest room, workers should supervise children of the same gender. When not possible, the worker should stay at the rest room door until the child is finished in the stall. Children should have as much privacy as possible when using the rest room. Workers may enter to assist only when absolutely necessary.

5. Changing diapers is to be done in a room with at least one other worker present. No child shall be left unattended on a changing table at any time.

6. Emergency evacuation procedures are clearly posted in every children's room. Workers are to guide children as a group to the designated safe area outside the building.

7. Children through kindergarten age are to be signed in and out by the same parent or other responsible adult. Parents are to be informed of this requirement when they first bring their children.

Sample Guidelines
for Discipline

1. Approach discipline situations as opportunities for learning, not as interruptions or distractions that keep you from teaching. Remember, "discipline" and "disciple" come from the same word and have the same core meaning.

2. Focus on the desired positive behaviors, not the undesirable actions. Thus, state classroom guidelines in positive, not negative, terms. (Instead of "No running indoors," say, "Walk when you're inside. Running is for outside.")

3. Establish clearly defined guidelines appropriate to the age level and the room. With each guideline, include a reason that children or youth can easily understand. Examples:

- Listen when others are speaking, so that everyone can hear and learn.
- Wait for your turn, so that everyone gets a chance to participate.
- Share supplies, snacks, space, etc., with everyone in the group, so no one is left out.
- Take good care of our supplies and equipment, so we can all use them.
- When you use something, put it back. When you make a mess, clean it up. This shows respect for each other and for our church building.
- Each person's drawing, writing, or answers may be different. That's one of the ways we know God made each one of us special.
- Work only on your own paper, drawing, or project so each of us can enjoy finishing his/her own work.
- (Preschool) When someone else has something you want, you may ask for it. When that person is done, it will be your turn.
- (Preschool) Blocks are for building, not for throwing or using as guns. We are learning about ways God wants us to be kind, so we have to be careful how we use things that might hurt someone.
- (Preschool) We can build as high as your shoulder. Then, if the blocks fall, no one will get hurt.
- (Children) You may sit next to anyone as long as you do not disturb others. It's important to be with your friends, and it's important to learn. Let's make sure we do both.

SAMPLE GUIDELINES FOR MINISTERING TO
Persons With Disabilities

If no persons with disabilities are now attending:

1. Survey the congregation and the community to identify persons with disabilities who are interested in attending.

2. Present the need to church leaders and secure support for initiating ministry efforts to persons with disabilities.

If at least one person with disabilities is now attending:

1. If at all possible, include persons with disabilities in regular groups. In general, the only reasons for placing a person in a special group is if his/her behavior is excessively disruptive to the group or if the person is unable to interact positively with others in the group.

2. Form a group to develop procedures to meet the special needs of each person with a disability. The group (a church staff member, an educator, a leader in the church's education program, parent of a child with disabilities, parent of a child without disabilities, a teacher) should focus on ways to accommodate the specific needs of each person. Open dialog among these people builds understanding, which is essential for success.

3. Provide opportunity, if needed, for persons with disabilities to receive orientation in advance of participating in a regular group. Personal or small group guidance is often very helpful on a continuing basis in addition to participation in a regular group.

4. Prepare the teachers for the special needs they will be helping to meet. Emphasize the person's abilities and interests, rather than sensationalizing the disability. In most cases where teachers already provide a variety of learning approaches, few modifications need be made to classroom procedures to accommodate a learner with disabilities. It is generally not necessary to give extensive training in anticipation of every possible problem that could arise. In many situations it is wise to enlist an additional teacher or aide to assist in the group, giving special attention as needed to the person with disabilities.

5. Prepare other group members for their part in creating an accepting, encouraging environment.

A helpful source for information about ministering to people with disabilities is the Christian Church Foundation for the Handicapped, P.O. Box 9869, Knoxville, TN 37940.

Sample Guidelines for Ministering to Persons With Disabilities

SAMPLE GUIDELINES FOR MINISTERING TO
Persons Infected With HIV

1. As much as possible, include HIV infected persons in regular groups. In general, the only reasons for restricting access to a group by a person infected with HIV is if he/she also has tuberculosis or open sores, or if he/she is at high risk from infections from others (i.e., during a flu or chicken pox epidemic). An adult, teen, or older child with HIV infection who is otherwise healthy poses no health threat to others in a church situation. Safety precautions that should be taken are:

- Everyone's blood—not just that of persons known to be infected by HIV— should be considered as possibly contagious. Any cuts or scrapes should be treated cautiously.
- Wear disposable latex gloves when giving first aid.
- Use disposable paper towels and a ten-percent bleach solution to clean any blood spills. (Bleach destroys the HIV virus.)
- Cover with a bandage any cut or scrape that may ooze blood.
- Place in a plastic bag all disposable items touched by blood, then tie the bag shut and place in a trash bin.
- Launder or dry-clean any clothes contacted by blood.
- After completing first aid, wash hands thoroughly with soap and water.

Children of preschool age and younger need additional consideration, since they are not yet capable of practicing safe personal hygiene. An infant, toddler, or preschooler infected with HIV can participate safely in a regular group if carefully monitored by a responsible adult enlisted and trained to stay with the child at all times. To lessen fears by other parents, this person should:

- Be fully aware of the ways in which HIV is and is not transmitted.
- Keep this child's bottle and toys away from other children, storing them as the child finishes with them so they can be thoroughly washed later.
- Be ready to intervene gently but firmly should the child show any aggressive behavior toward other children.
- Change the child's diapers. Those changing any child's diapers:
    May wear disposable latex gloves;
    Must clean the changing area with ten-percent bleach solution;
    Must thoroughly wash hands with soap and water.

2. Form a group to develop procedures to meet the special needs of each person or persons infected with HIV. The group (a church staff member, a medical professional, a leader in the church's education program, person infected with HIV or a family member, a person not infected, a teacher in the program attended by the person infected with HIV) should focus on ways the church's ministries can accommodate the specific needs of a person infected with HIV. Open dialog among people builds understanding, which is essential for success.

3. Provide orientation for persons infected with HIV, and/or their parents, in advance of participating in a regular group. Personal and/or small group guidance is often very helpful on a continuing basis in addition to participation in a regular group.

4. Prepare the teachers for the special needs they will be helping to meet. Emphasize the abilities and interests of the person infected with HIV, rather than sensationalizing the disease. In most cases, few modifications need be made to classroom procedures to accommodate a learner infected with HIV.

A helpful source for information about ministering to people with HIV infections is Heart to Heart, Inc., 2115 SE Adams, Milwaukie, OR 97222-7773 Also, the book, *The AIDS Epidemic: Balancing Compassion and Justice* , by John E. Dietrich, M.D. and Glenn G. Wood, M.D. (Multnomah Press, 1990), addresses both theological, social, and medical issues related to AIDS.

Sample Guidelines for Ministering to Persons Infected With HIV

7
Enlisting and Equipping Volunteers

esus knew that eager volunteers are scarce: "The harvest is plentiful but the workers are few" (Matthew 9:37).

You may be the most recent Christian leader to regret the same lack; you are unlikely the last. Perhaps the most urgent challenge facing the church's educational ministries in the twenty-first century is that of enlisting and equipping enough volunteers to carry out the great challenge of reaching and teaching.

Jesus' statement suggests three important principles.

Recruiting Maxim #1: *When seeking to involve people in ministry, focus on the needs in people's lives, not the needs of your program.*

Jesus expressed his concern about workers immediately after he saw crowds of followers "harassed and helpless, like sheep without a shepherd" (v. 36). Their need, not his program, motivated his recruiting concern. Administrators often fall into the trap of allowing organizational needs to motivate their recruiting efforts.

"I've got to line up three more teachers before the board meeting next Tuesday."

"It sure wouldn't look good for our church to have to shut down that program because of a staffing shortage."

"If I can just get two more people signed on, it'll be a big load off my shoulders."

In contrast, Jesus' concern was motivated by his compassion for those who needed to be taught and loved.

Recruiting Maxim #2: *When seeking to involve people in ministry, ask God to supply the right people.*

Jesus gave specific instructions on what to do about a staff shortage: "Ask the Lord of the harvest, therefore, to send out workers into his harvest field" (v. 38).

The beginning point of any recruiting effort must be prayer, specifically asking the "Lord of the harvest" to provide the workers necessary. Since God, as "Lord of the harvest," cares greatly about those who need to be reached and taught, this is not a request he will regard lightly. When asking someone to enlist in a spiritual ministry, the whole process must begin from a spiritual foundation.

Recruiting Maxim #3: *When seeking to involve people in ministry, help the present workers to succeed.*

Jesus' immediate action in recognition of a staff shortage was to send out the workers he had.

Matthew wrote these words of Jesus directly before Jesus called his twelve disciples and instructed them on their ministry (Matthew 10). Luke records the same words as part of Jesus' instructions to seventy-two other disciples that he sent out to nearby towns (Luke 10).

Administrators need to guard against letting a staff shortage get in the way of developing those who have already enlisted. The best way to draw new people into ministry is to equip those already serving so that they succeed in their ministries. Few people will ever want to sign on with a group of people who are struggling and defeated. But a group of people who are accomplishing something worthwhile are powerfully effective in attracting others to get involved.

Clarify Objectives and Responsibilities

Chapter 6 provided guidelines for defining the various roles people fill in education ministries. Clear, simple written statements (for every ministry position) ensure that everyone involved knows both the purpose and the procedures of a particular position. The ideal time to review a position is when a new person is being considered for that position. Clarify and update the stated goals of the job and the specific actions that must be done in order to accomplish those goals.

If church leaders are vague about what a particular job entails, the person being asked to do the job will also be unclear about what to do. This vagueness results in dissatisfaction with how the job is done because the job performance will not meet anyone's expectations.

Often, it is helpful to review a job description with the person who has been doing the job. Invite this person's evaluation by asking questions such as:

- Which of the functions listed took the most time to do? the least time?
- If you were going to continue in this ministry for another year, what statements would you change?
- Which actions produced the most satisfaction for you? the most frustration?
- Which actions were most important in helping to reach the goals of this position? the least important?

When defining what is being asked of a volunteer, list specific statements indicating what the church will provide to support the person in fulfilling his/her responsibilities. Include items such as:

- Training opportunities (when and how often);
- Resources and supplies (what materials are available);
- Team support (who will work alongside and who can be contacted for help).

Identify People With Potential

"Our church is so small, we don't have enough qualified people to cover the jobs that need to be done."

"Our church is so big, no one knows how to find those who would work."

"The people who know the kinds of people we need are so involved with the people we have, they don't know the people we don't have."

"Our leaders have been doing this ministry so long, they've run out of people they haven't already approached half a dozen times."

"Our leaders are so new, they don't know the people who might be interested in serving."

Whatever the size or situation of your church, you are bound to find that one of the most difficult aspects of recruiting is deciding whom to ask. No one wants to spend an evening making phone calls to people who have no interest or inclination to get involved. Every church needs a well-thought-out plan for identifying people who have the potential to be effective in ministry. Following are three key components of such a plan.

Ministry Coordinator

A significant innovation in many churches has been the designation of an individual or group assigned to gather and coordinate information about people's abilities, backgrounds, and concerns (the A, B, Cs of recruiting information). A ministry coordinator (committee) is independent of any specific program. He/she works with the leaders of all programs, sharing and evaluating information about people. Significant advances in computer software for churches provide efficient means of updating and retrieving a wide variety of ministry-related information about people.

Sometimes, the ministry coordinator is responsible for disseminating information to the congregation about ministry opportunities.

Preliminary Screening

Whether done by a ministry coordinator or by program leaders, great value exists in making periodic, low-threat contacts with people to discover those with abilities, background, and concerns related to educational ministries. This can be done through a variety of means in which the purpose is not to fill slots, but to discover information.

Written Survey. Asking people to fill out a form identifying their abilities, backgrounds, and concerns has had mixed value over the years. If given to the entire congregation at one time, many churches find that by the time they sift through all the paperwork and start trying to use the information, a good deal of it is already out of date. People in the congregation tend to feel slighted if they mark something, and hope to be contacted, and nothing comes of it. However, there are many advantages of a thoughtfully designed survey, one that does not try to cover every possible ministry the church might ever conceive of doing.

The sample survey on pages 157-159 shows more categories and fields than you will need. Before using this survey, determine which categories and subfields really will be of use to you. Then, eliminate the others from the survey.

Class. Most churches periodically offer classes that help people indicate their abilities and their openness to chosen areas of service. Even adult Sunday school classes are useful for gaining information about people and their potential for ministry involvement.

Interview. Personal conversations with people, either by phone or in person, are also valuable ways of discovering relevant information about people's involvement.

Information gathered about people is then made available to those seeking people for specific ministry positions.

Referrals

The people who are already involved in a ministry are often excellent sources of information about people who could be effective in that ministry area. Simply ask from time to time, "Who do you know in the congregation who could do a good job at what you are doing?" Do not ask, "Who do you know who is interested?" By and large, the people who have expressed an interest are already involved. Besides, it's best not to eliminate consideration of people with potential without giving them the chance to consider an opportunity for ministry.

Approval

Once someone has been suggested as a possible volunteer, a specified individual or group must decide whether or not to invite that person to get involved.

If several people have been identified as potentials to contact for a particular position, a decision must be made about whom to contact first.

If numerous positions need to be filled, numerous people need approval.

"Official" approval of potential candidates protects the church, saves time, and gives additional authority to the person making the contact. It is far stronger to say to a prospect, "Our Christian Education Board voted for me to approach you," than to merely say, "I thought it would be a good idea to ask."

Present the Challenge and the Team

"You wouldn't really be interested in teaching three-year-olds, would you?"

This negative approach will most likely talk a potential candidate out of ministry. By the way that they present a task, some well-intentioned leaders contribute to negative responses. A negative approach may be caused by the urgent need to get a position filled or by not taking time to think through how best to present a need. Whatever the cause, a negative approach results in an ineffective invitation.

Many administrators also make a mistake when they try to make jobs sound exceedingly easy, with such a minimal time commitment that people would hardly even know they have taken on the task. Such an approach is a mistake for three reasons.

1) No job is ever that easy.

2) People tend to do what they agree to do—and no more. Should the person agree to take the position, he/she is likely to put in only the amount of time and effort mentioned when this "easy" job was presented.

3) People are not motivated by "easy, minimal-commitment" tasks. Why should a person give any time at all to a job that sounds so condescendingly simple?

Recruiting Maxim #4: *People rarely perform above the level to which they were recruited.*

People respond to a challenge, especially when it involves being part of a team effort. Therefore, leaders should present ministry opportunities as significant, worthwhile endeavors that will bring out the best in those who pursue them.

General Notices

General announcements and information about a ministry are important parts of any approach to a potential worker. This information colors a person's attitude about that ministry.

If the first thing a person hears about a ministry is a request to get involved, a positive response is unlikely.

If the first *good* thing a person hears about a ministry is a request to get involved, a positive response is *really* unlikely.

An ongoing program of communicating the goals and accomplishments of the educational ministries is a vital part of the recruiting process. While few people are likely to volunteer because of a notice in the bulletin or an announcement from the pulpit, those messages contribute significantly to a person's receptivity at the time a personal contact is made.

Personal Contacts

Once a person has been approved for ministry, the following components should be part of the contact process.

- Determine who will contact the person. Two people should be involved in the contact. One of these contacts should be a person who is on the ministry team that the new person would join.
- Send a letter. A brief letter allows a person to respond in private before having to talk to a real person. Mention the general area of ministry for which the person has been approved and indicate when a follow-up contact will be made to explain the ministry fully. Ask the person to begin praying to determine if this ministry is where God wants him/her to serve.
- Several days later, make a telephone call. At this point, you have three options.
  1. Ask the person to choose a convenient time to meet so you can explain the ministry opportunity.
  2. Invite the person to observe a session of the group you want him/her to consider. Meet after the session to discuss the person's involvement. Observation of a ministry group in action is generally most effective when a person has been briefed ahead of time on what to look for. (*See the "Observation" section below.*)
  3. Ask if this is a convenient time for you to explain the ministry opportunity. If not, schedule a time to call again. When time is of the essence or when dealing with a congregation whose people are spread over a wide distance, it is most efficient to do as much as possible over the phone.
- Explain the ministry and the specific position you want this person to consider. In doing so, focus on these seven things:
  1. The objectives of the ministry (why this position is important);

2. The specific ministry position and its major responsibilities (what the candidate is being asked to do);

3. The length of the term of service (when and for how long the candidate will do it);

4. The reasons this person was selected to be asked (why we believe the candidate can succeed in this position);

5. The others on the ministry team (whom the candidate will work with);

6. The resources available (what the candidate will be given);

7. The process (how to make the right decision).

If talking to someone about a position involving children or youth, also explain the church's child and youth safety policies. If in a face-to-face meeting, show the main curriculum resources now being used.

Emphasize that your objective is to find someone who not only can do the job, but who will benefit and grow through it as well. Ask the person not to decide one way or another until he/she has had a chance to observe the group in action and has prayed about it for at least several days. In most cases, it is best for everyone involved if a person does not make a quick decision but takes time to consider fully what is involved.

Observation

Few people would buy a car without at least seeing it, if not giving it a test drive. Similarly, give people an opportunity to watch other people doing what they are being asked to do. Except in very small rooms, an observer usually has little or no impact on what goes on in the group, especially once it becomes a familiar practice to teachers and learners.

Provide copies of the curriculum resources for the person to follow along with as the session progresses.

Make sure that the group being observed is a good example of the ministry you want the prospect to do. If the specific group for which you are seeking a new person is not functioning very well, have the prospect observe a similar group that does demonstrate positive skills and attitudes.

The observation guidelines on page 160 will help make an observation session valuable for a person's decision about his/her involvement.

Secure the Commitment

Once a person has been introduced to the ministry goals and procedures and has had an opportunity to observe a group in action, take a positive approach in bringing the person to a decision.

1. Pray with the person and get him/her to agree to pray further for at least several days.

2. Ask the person to talk with family members about the responsibilities this position will involve.

3. Explain that it may be necessary for the person to shuffle some priorities. Most teaching and leading positions in an educational ministry are not conducive to being tacked on at the end of an already busy schedule. To be effective in making an impact on people's lives, such a position must be put near the top of the priority list.

4. Give the person an information form (pages 161 and 162) to complete after deciding to get involved. If the decision is not to get involved at this time, the application can be discarded. Explain the following:

- The information form is confidential. (Identify the people who will read it.)
- It is a positive expression of the church's commitment to provide a safe and healthy environment for children, young people, and adults.
- The references given on it will be contacted.
- A decision not to get involved at the present time in no way implies that a person did not want to complete the form.

Some people resist using an information form, feeling it puts an added barrier in front of people who are already difficult enough to enlist. Experience shows that an information form shows that the church takes this ministry seriously, thus enhancing people's sense of its value. Rarely, if ever, does an information form deter someone who would be truly effective in such a ministry.

Equip for Success

Training Maxim #1: *Each local church has been given the gifts needed to carry out its ministry of equipping the saints (Ephesians 4).*

Once a person accepts a ministry responsibility, the work begins to provide the new worker with the knowledge, skills, and motivation needed to be effective. Leaders who give minimal attention to this process must subscribe to one or more of these flawed theories.

- Teaching or leading is easy; anyone can do it, especially since our curriculum is so easy to use.
- Our standards are so high that the only people we recruit are ones who are already skilled.

- Our church is uniquely blessed by having a very high percentage of capable people who were trained by (choose one: some other church they used to attend; IBM, General Motors, AT&T, or the Army; regularly watching Christian television; a lifetime of attending church and listening to sermons).
- Leaving people on their own after they're recruited is a great way to separate the wheat from the chaff. The ones who survive are the only ones we really want.
- Of course, we're big on training! We sent eight of our teachers to a Sunday school convention last fall.
- We could have as good a program as (insert name of another church) if only some capable people like they have would start coming to our church.
- We don't have anyone qualified to lead training, so we just do the best we can without it.
- We had a training seminar last year, so we're going to take a year or two off and emphasize other things.
- We'd like to train our people better, but our leaders are too busy leading, and besides, it's too hard to get people to come to training meetings.

A church that will have a quality educational ministry in the twenty-first century must have a strong commitment to developing and supporting people who will carry out its teaching ministry. No one else will equip the leaders and teachers a church needs. While special events such as Sunday school conventions can be very helpful for motivation and disseminating ideas, the real work of helping people become skilled must be done on an ongoing basis within the life of the church where people serve.

An effective training program involves a combination of many approaches:

- One-to-one interaction about ways to improve;
- Regular meetings in which the people involved share ideas and plan the specific actions they will take;
- Ongoing observation and evaluation;
- Periodic training workshops or seminars;
- Individual and group use of supportive resources (training videos, audio cassettes, magazines, books, etc.).

When considering how to provide these experiences for people, it is helpful to begin by looking at the process from the perspective of the newly enlisted volunteer. What needs to be done to get this person off to a good start? What actions will build a new person's confidence and enable him/her to have a positive sense of accomplishment?

Initial Orientation

Most organizations develop a host of insider terms and procedures that everyone knows but never thinks to pass on to a new person. Many of these a new person doesn't know enough to ask about until the need arises, and then it may be too late. Consider a brief walk-through orientation that introduces a new staff member to basic survival information.

People. Church people, especially very involved church people, are notorious for assuming everyone already knows everyone else. Take time to introduce a new staff volunteer, not just to those on his/her immediate ministry team, but to all others he/she is likely to contact either formally or informally. This includes the people working in the rooms next door and across the hall, the nice lady who has the key to the supply room, the quiet gentleman who slips in and picks up the roster and offering every week, the custodian who sets up the room on Saturday, and so on. People feel comfortable in a situation when they know the people.

Places. Don't assume that someone who has never taught three-year-olds will automatically know where things are. Point out where the nearest rest rooms are (both for adults and for children), the drinking fountains, the supply room, the library, the Sunday school office, the emergency escape route, a telephone, and so on. Even though this person is not going to be made responsible for a certain function (e.g., getting the snack supplies from the church kitchen), make him/her aware of how to do it. When the person who does that function is not there and someone asks the new volunteer to fill in, he/she will know what to do.

Policies and Procedures. Provide a printed copy of all policies and procedures—not just the ones related to teaching. What is the policy about turning off the lights? Who checks that windows and doors are locked? Are there any activities that are not permitted in the rooms (e.g., no sand)? What happens to personal items that are left in the rooms?

Program. The above items all sound somewhat peripheral to the purposes of the program, but they are important pieces of information to help a new person feel at home. However, it is even more important to have a plan for introducing a new volunteer to the operations of the ministry, and specifically, his/her part in it.

Provide Direction

Make a point of emphasizing what the program is trying to accomplish. A new person may already feel strongly drawn to work toward the objectives of the ministry or may have agreed to work primarily because of a desire to get involved in something worthwhile, a sense of responsibility to help out, or because the children are so cute. These are not wrong reasons. But if the basic goals of the ministry are not clearly communicated to new staff up front, those objectives will be little more than nice thoughts inscribed on official documents. And if the program's purposes are not regularly reinforced with the whole staff, what actually happens will have little resemblance to your vision for this ministry.

Demonstrate Resources

"Look in the TM for your BLAs. Sometimes they need the S book and sometimes they use something from the TR."

If the above quote makes any sense at all to you, you've probably spent considerable time around Sunday school curriculum. But to a person just getting started, the jargon in that quote is gibberish. (Translation: TM=teacher manual; BLAs=Bible learning activities; S book=student book; TR=teaching resources.)

It takes only ten or fifteen minutes to give a new volunteer a hands-on introduction to the essential curriculum materials he/she will use. Emphasize and explain these items in the teacher manual.

- Lesson aims tell us why we're teaching the lesson and what we plan for learners to accomplish by the end of the session.

- Lesson focus statement is the one important truth we want every learner to remember.
- Session schedule is how we divide the time during the session. Each segment is important because it contributes to a balanced learning experience.
- Learning activities are ideas that suggest ways to involve learners actively to accomplish the learning aims.
- Lesson content (Bible story, etc.) contains the information we will present or help learners discover, always making sure it leads up to or reinforces understanding of the lesson focus statement.

Show where the related curriculum pieces (student book, teaching resources, etc.) are referred to and what their function is in stimulating interest, clarifying or simplifying information, and guiding towards life application.

Schedule Observation

Training Maxim #2: *People teach they way they were taught.*

The new person who has been enlisted to serve has a mental image, part conscious and a large part unconscious, of how to go about doing his/her new job. This mental image is the result of a lifetime of experience in various teaching/learning and leading/following situations. These experiences reach back into childhood. Any resemblance between this mental image and the way in which church leaders believe the ministry should be carried out is often purely coincidental.

The best way to provide a new person with a better mental image of how to do this ministry effectively is to plan opportunities for each new person to observe an experienced, skillful person in action. Just as the prospective worker watched others at work as part of the recruiting process, similar observations are needed to help a new volunteer become familiar and comfortable with effective ministry procedures.

Limit First Assignments

Along with the opportunity to observe someone else in action, plan a limited number of low-threat functions this new person can do to get started.

- Choose assignments that are simple so the person is able to complete the task successfully. (Teaching a new hymn to middle schoolers is definitely *not* in the simple category.)
- Choose assignments that are interesting so the person is intrigued and motivated. (Punching out dozens of stickers for a craft project does *not* qualify.)
- Choose assignments that are relational, allowing the new person to interact with learners in the group. (Running to the church kitchen to get extra cups for refreshments does *not* fit this criteria.)

The new person could work alongside an experienced worker or do another task where an experienced person is available to observe and assist, if needed. As the person gradually becomes more familiar and confident, additional, more-challenging tasks can be added.

Develop Skills

Some people are naturals. Give them a job, a little direction, then turn them loose. From the very first try, they seem to do it right. Then there are the rest of us.

How do you equip someone with skills they do not already have? Follow these guidelines.

1. Begin by focusing on what the person already does well, not on the areas that need improvement. Affirm a person for numerous positives before mentioning a single area where improvement could be made.

2. Set an example of seeking to grow, by asking the new person for suggestions on what you could have done differently or better in some area of your ministry. If the other person has no suggestions to offer, be ready with a few of your own, clearly pointing out things you want to do better next time.

3. Invite the person to critique his/her own efforts. Ask questions such as: What did you feel most comfortable doing? When did you feel things were not going as smoothly as you would have liked? What do you think you might do differently next time? A person is far more likely to work at improving in an area he/she recognizes as a weakness than in one that is pointed out by someone else.

4. Limit any suggested improvements to one at a time. No one can improve on multiple fronts simultaneously. Encourage the person to be specific in describing actions to take for improving. Don't accept a vague hope to do better next time.

5. Suggest practicing a skill at home in front of a mirror or a family member. A tape recorder is a great tool for practicing giving directions, asking questions, telling a story, explaining the purpose of an activity, and so on.

6. As time passes, affirm the person for signs of growth.

7. If a person really struggles with a specific skill (e.g., asking good questions), help the person find a way to simplify the function (e.g., Instead of trying to ask four or five questions, focus on just one or two.) Observe the person in action and identify one specific way in which he/she

can improve (e.g., Ask one *why* question in each lesson as a way to encourage learners to think about meaning, not just facts.). Should difficulty in mastering a specific skill become a barrier to continued growth, suggest that someone else do that function for awhile.

Arrange Support

Everyone needs encouragement and the friendship that grows from shared involvement in ministry. The best way to help a volunteer make a good beginning in a new ministry is to link that person with others who are engaged in the same or similar efforts. Jesus set the pattern for this aspect of training when he sent his disciples out in pairs.

However, when discussing leadership teams in Chapter 6, it was shown that a team is not simply two or more people who happen to be doing the same or a similar task. Even doing a task at the same time in the same room does not mean the people are a supportive team. A true ministry team exists when the following occur:

- People meet together often enough to get to know one another as individuals.
- Team members plan together what they are going to do and encourage and assist each other in doing their tasks.
- A climate is established for honest sharing about both personal and ministry needs, and team members faithfully pray for each other.
- Team members are able to laugh and cry together.

Communicate Appreciation

"Why should I compliment teachers and leaders for doing what they're supposed to do?" an administrator asked. "They should be doing it for the Lord, not to get noticed."

This administrator was technically right, but at the same time, very, very wrong.

Just as people need love, they also need encouragement and affirmation—especially when they are tackling a new responsibility. Thoughtfully express appreciation. Comment about something done well. Even a few sincere words can be powerfully effective in building a sense of satisfaction and achievement in doing a job.

While a general word of appreciation or commendation is nice to receive, a volunteer who is learning a new job needs very specific affirmation that points out what he/she has done well.

Instead of saying only: "Glad to have you with us."

Also say: "Your enthusiasm gives everyone a real boost."

Instead of saying only: "Nice work."

Also say: "You do so well maintaining eye contact with class members while you're talking."

Instead of saying only: "The students really like you."

Also say: "Your smile is contagious. People really respond to it."

Instead of saying only: "Good job."

Also say: "It's so helpful that you're here a little early."

Instead of saying only: "I really appreciate your doing this."

Also say: "I can tell you were well prepared."

Removing a Member From the Team

"Since Jesus said we should ask the Lord of the harvest to send workers into the harvest, would it be all right to also ask him to send a few workers out of the harvest?" This question by a harried administrator reflects one of the most difficult challenges in ministry: how to "fire" a volunteer.

Reasons for Removal

The difficult, even painful, process of removing a person from a ministry position is sometimes necessary for one of several reasons:

Inability to do the job. Sometimes a person simply lacks the skills or knowledge needed for the task. Sometimes a person just does not have enough time to serve effectively. A person whose best efforts are ineffective may be doing more harm than good. Unfortunately, sometimes the person is unaware of his/her shortcomings and truly thinks all is well.

Unwillingness to do essential tasks. For example, a person may enjoy "being with the children," but is unwilling to prepare adequately or participate in planning or training opportunities. The volunteer may not share the leadership's view of the importance of certain tasks, and this hinders efforts to reach ministry goals. Reluctance to do what is needed is a common sign of burnout, a loss of motivation resulting from stress, overcommitment, or even boredom.

Undependability. A person may have plenty of ability, knowledge, and time, and may agree that certain functions are important. But these are not enough if he/she cannot be counted on to do the job.

Dissension. A volunteer with a negative attitude can obstruct the efforts of everyone else involved in a ministry, even causing divisions among the others who serve.

Doctrinal disagreements. The teaching ministry of the church is the last place a person should serve who disagrees with important church teachings.

Moral/ethical problems. Sadly, Sunday school teachers and other Christian education workers are not immune to immorality.

Guidelines

Dealing with such problems in the church's education ministries is especially sensitive because of the tremendous impact teachers and leaders have on other people who look to them as examples. However, the responsible administrator must be concerned not only about the group and its members, but also about the well-being of the volunteer. The church that has enlisted a person into a ministry position has a responsibility to help that person if he/she fails in fulfilling that ministry.

When a personnel problem arises, the administrative team generally has four options to prayerfully consider:

1. Try to correct the problem so the person can continue successfully on the ministry team. Thus, if the person lacks skill or knowledge, the administrator must determine if that skill or knowledge can be provided. If the person is unmotivated to do essential tasks, can the leader successfully encourage a change of attitude? And are you sure the worker fully understands the requirements for the job he/she has taken? In far too many cases, the lack of ability or knowledge is the direct result of the church having failed to provide adequate training for ministry. If no leader has ever pointed out ways to do better, it is unfair to expect the volunteer to have made those improvements.

2. Move the person to a more suitable

area of ministry. Often a change to another place of service can produce very successful results. For example, a teacher who has taught the same age level for many years and no longer shows much enthusiasm may get a new infusion of energy when given the opportunity to teach teenagers or adults. Or a person who has been frustrated in a leadership position may relish the opportunity to serve as a teacher.

3. Clarify and emphasize the requirements of the job, allowing the person the option to either improve his/her performance or resign. This approach needs to be varied slightly depending on whether or not these requirements were clearly understood when the person began to serve.

If the requirements for the position have changed since the person got involved, it is necessary to admit that a change has been made. It is not fair to hold a person responsible for actions he/she did not agree to do when enlisted. But, a clear case must be presented for why these requirements have been instituted. This frees a person to decide whether or not to continue without feeling the stigma of failure.

If the requirements for the position have been well known from the beginning, affirm the person for wanting to do an effective job, then stress the need for those required functions to be fulfilled. A straightforward question to ask is, "Based on your experience in this position and your present circumstances, will you be able to start fulfilling these requirements?" If the answer is "No," the response called for is, "Thank you for your honesty and for all the time and energy you have contributed. I know you understand how important these requirements are, so we'll start looking for someone who can take over for you as soon as possible."

Depending on the reason the person is being removed, you may either make the change immediately, or ask, "Would you continue on an interim basis until we find a suitable replacement?"

4. Dismiss the person from the ministry position. If none of the first three options works, or if the administrative team deems the situation so serious as to require immediate termination, then the person must be told face-to-face that he/she may not continue in that position. In carrying out this difficult task:

- Prayerfully prepare a written statement of the reason for the dismissal, presenting it in terms of the ministry's written goals and job descriptions. (It is wise to have this statement officially approved by the administrative team, entering it into the minutes of the group or its confidential personnel records.)

- Have two members of the administrative team present, as tangible evidence that this action is taken on behalf of the full leadership, not as a personal matter between the volunteer and one leader.

- Clearly state the reason for the dismissal.

- Affirm the person's efforts and intentions, and leave the door open for possible future service.

- After the meeting, write a brief report of the meeting to be signed by both administrative team members who were present. Submit the report to the administrative team.

In any personnel action that may be seen as disciplinary, it is wise to confer with church leaders responsible for personnel decisions. It may also be prudent to consult with legal counsel to ensure that the rights and confidentiality of the volunteer are protected and to avoid unforeseen problems or recriminations.

Sample Church
Family Survey

Personal Information

Name: _____ Title: ____ Nickname: _____

Address: _____ Gender: ❏M ❏F

City: _____ State: _____ Zip: _____

Home Phone _____ ❏ Unlisted? Work Phone _____

Relationship to church (mark one):

❏ Sunday school only   ❏ Church member   ❏ Spouse of member
❏ Child of member   ❏ Regular attender ❏ Visitor

Date of first visit to church _____

Reason for visit: _____

Date baptized _____ Where baptized _____

Date new member class _____

Date added to this congregation: _____

Added by (mark one):   ❏ Transfer   ❏ Baptism

Marital status (mark one):

❏ Single   ❏ Married   ❏ Engaged
❏ Divorced   ❏ Widowed   ❏ Separated

Spouse: _____

Children living at home: _____

_____

Occupational status: (mark one):

❏ Employed   ❏ Self-Employed ❏ Unemployed
❏ Student   ❏ Homemaker   ❏ Retired

Occupational title: _____

Other

Birthday: _____ Wedding anniversary: _____

Care group: _____ Envelope number: _____

Sunday school class: _____ Class position: _____

GROUPS/SKILLS/INTERESTS

1=Active
2=Experienced
3=Trained
4=Interested

Check all that apply.

GROUPS
__Sanctuary choir
__Children's choir
__Youth choir
__Bible study
__Men's group
__Women's group
__Boy Scouts
__Girl Scouts

ADMIN/ PROMO
__Elder
__Trustee
__Deacon
__Finance com.
__Property com.
__Personnel com.
__Nominating
__Secretary
__Typist
__Bookkeeper
__Artist
__Writer/Editor

WORSHIP
__Usher/Greeter
__Sound tech.
__Music com.
__Worship com.
__Banners

EDUCATION
__Bible study ldr
__Teach preschool
__Teach children
__Teach youth
__Teach adults
__Usher/Greeter
__Ch. Ed. com.
__Day School Bd.
__Librarian
__Sunday school
__Weeknights
__VBS

OUTREACH/ MISSIONS
__Missions com.
__Evangelism com.
__Visitation
__Member. com.
__Community ser.
__Telephoning

FELLOWSHIP
__Fellowship com.
__Kitchen com.
__Helping

COMMUNITY SERVICES
__Disaster aid
__Foster home
__Elderly
__Hosp. volunteer
__Literacy aid
__Local govt.
__School board
__Youth work

VEHICLES
__Bicycle
__Bus
__Motorcycle
__Motor home
__Off-road
__Pickup
__Truck
__Boat

PROMOTION
__Advertising
__Poster/Art
__Public relations
__Public speaking
__Publicity/Edit
__Sign painting
__TV/Radio
__Writing

BUSINESS
__Administration
__Banking
__Bookkeeping
__Clerk
__Mail room
__Office manager
__Purchasing
__Receptionist
__Sales
__Secretary
__Typist

DEVELOPMENT
__Estate planning
__Investments
__Foundations

PROFESSIONAL
__Architect
__Clergy
__Contractor
__Counselor
__Engineer
__Financial
__Legal
__Medical/Dental
__System analyst
__Teacher

**Sample Church
Family Survey
2**

1=Active
2=Experienced
3=Trained
4=Interested

Check all that apply.

TECHNICAL
__Audio Visual
__Computer oper.
__Driver
__Lighting
__Mechanic
__Printer
__Sound
__Typesetting
__Video

REPAIR/ CONST
__Carpenter
__Carpet layer
__Electrician
__Gardener
__Handyman
__Glazier
__Janitor
__Landscaper
__Mason
__Painter
__Plumber

VOCAL MUSIC
__Soprano
__Alto
__Tenor
__Bass
__Soloist
__Small group
__Teacher
__Director

INSTRU. MUSIC
__Piano
__Organ
__Strings
__Woodwind
__Brass
__Percussion
__Guitar
__Bagpipes
__Teacher
__Director

CHILD CARE
__Church nursery
__In homes
__In own home
__Transportation
__Days
__Evenings
__Weekends
__Teenager

KITCHEN
__Baking
__Chef
__Clean-up
__Decorations
__Meal planning
__Receptions
__Serving

DRAMA
__Acting
__Choreography
__Costume design
__Directing
__Make-up
__Set construction
__Set design
__Sewing costume
__Stage crew
__Narrator

CAMPING
__Backpacking
__Camping
__Rock climbing
__First aid
__Group leader
__Life guard
__Retreat plan.

LANGUAGES
__Teach English
__Arabic
__Armenian
__Chinese
__French
__German
__Greek
__Hebrew
__Sign language
__Spanish

CRAFTS/ PHOTO
__Floral arrange.
__Artist
__Develop film
__Group crafts
__Macramé
__Video
__Sewing
__Photography

INDIV. SPORTS
__Coach
__Archery
__Boating
__Fishing
__Golf
__Hunting
__Jogging
__Sailing
__Scuba
__Snow skiing
__Swimming
__Water skiing

TEAM SPORTS
__Coach
__Baseball
__Basketball
__Bowling
__Football
__Racquetball
__Soccer
__Softball
__Tennis
__Volleyball

Sample Church
Family Survey
3

Observation
Guidelines

1. Arrive about fifteen minutes before the official starting time. This will allow you to ask a few questions and get comfortably settled before most learners arrive.

2. Bring a few sheets of blank paper, a pen or pencil, and a hard writing surface (i.e., a clipboard) to use in writing notes about what you see and hear and to record questions you would like to ask later.

3. Find an inconspicuous place to sit where you can hear and see easily.

4. Avoid the temptation to initiate conversation with learners or teachers during the session. This helps keep the learners focused on what the teacher is having them do, and it helps you see as typical a session as possible. It's OK to smile at someone who smiles at you, but then shift your eyes to the teacher or somewhere else in the room.

If a learner speaks to you, respond as briefly as possible, then suggest that he/she returns to what the rest of the class is doing.

5. Do everything possible to stifle the urge to laugh at any cute or humorous things learners say or do, unless of course, the whole group is laughing.

6. The basic idea is to be natural and relaxed without drawing undue attention to yourself.

7. During the session, look particularly for these things:

- Things the teachers do that you think you can do;
- Things the teachers do that you think you may not be able to do;
- Evidence of anything meaningful being accomplished;
- Items you have questions about.

8. After the session, meet with one or more of the staff to ask questions about what you saw and heard and to ask any other questions about the program.

Information Form

This form is to be completed by all persons who work in any educational ministry in our church.

Personal

Name _____ Phone _____

Address _____

City _____ State _____ Zip _____

Marital Status:: ☐ Single ☐ Married ☐ Divorced

Spouse Name _____

Children Names/Ages _____

_____

Occupation

Where employed? _____ Phone _____

Can you receive calls at work? ☐ Yes ☐ No   Hours? _____

Personal References (not a relative)

Name _____ Phone _____

Relationship _____

Address _____

Name _____ Phone _____

Relationship _____

Address _____

Have you read our church's policies on child and youth safety and protection against abuse? ☐ Yes ☐ No

What questions do you have about these policies?

Have you ever been convicted or pleaded guilty to child abuse or a crime involving actual or attempted sexual molestation of a minor? ☐ Yes ☐ No

If yes, please explain.

Is there any other information that we should know?

Faith and Church Involvement

1. When did you become a Christian? Describe the circumstances that led you to Christ.

This form is to be completed by all persons who work in any educational ministry in our church.

2. In your present Christian walk, who is Jesus Christ to you?

3. How long have you attended this church? _____

4. Are you currently a member? ☐ Yes ☐ No   How long? _____

5. What other church(es) have you regularly attended over the past three years?

6. What experiences in the church or community have you had in teaching or leading?

7. What factors (experiences, gifts, training, etc.) have contributed to your interest in teaching or leading?

8. What age group and what type of ministry would you prefer?

   first choice _____

   second choice _____

9. What are your greatest concerns and apprehensions as you contemplate this ministry?

Statement

The above information is true and correct to the best of my knowledge. I authorize any of the listed churches and references to give you any information they may have regarding my character and fitness to work in educational ministries.

Signature _____ Date _____

**Information Form
2**

8
Facilities, Furnishings, and Technology

The Classroom of the Twenty-First Century

In the mid-twentieth century, such a title would have awakened futuristic images in which technological marvels delivered vast amounts of knowledge, creating highly intelligent, wise, and moral learners.

During the closing decades of the century, social upheaval, inflationary spirals, and deep cuts in education budgets combined to change the expectations of many people. The continuing increase in the cost of maintaining or replacing aging buildings changed the vision for a facility of the future from one of shining, stimulating surroundings to high-maintenance buildings marked by grime and graffiti.

Public school systems are often dominated by this pessimistic view of the future. At the same time, many churches struggle with similar problems. If a congregation has not been led to recognize the high value of educational, nurturing ministries for all age levels, facilities for these programs are likely to be overlooked in the expenditure of funds.

While it is possible to conduct excellent educational ministries with inadequate facilities, several features in any facility significantly influence the quality of the learning experiences.

To provide a facility that effectively aids your church's ministry, four questions must be asked and carefully answered for the total church and for each ministry that uses the church's facilities.

1. What is our purpose in this community?

2. Whom are we trying to reach, and who is available to do this ministry?

3. What kinds of programs will accomplish our purpose for those people?

4. What kinds of facilities are needed for the operation of those programs?

General Facility Requirements

Because of the solid nature of buildings, there is a common tendency to let them shape the programs that are conducted inside them. Walls, ceilings, and floors create more than the physical parameters where groups go about their business. These borders establish limitations on both the size and type of programs a church offers. They often narrow the church's vision of what they can do in their reaching and teaching efforts.

To avoid being boxed in by the constraints of a building, church leaders must regularly examine whether they are allowing the facility to shape their ministry or letting their ministry shape their facilities.

The worksheet on pages 169 and 170 is helpful for examining facilities.

Room Specifications

In the early part of the twentieth century, the most common floor plan for Sunday school rooms was an assembly area with various small classrooms grouped around the sides. That pattern has given way to larger, open classrooms.

This change in building design allows teachers to work as teams, rather than being isolated in separate cubicles. The same change made student participation and choices much more efficient than the enclosed spaces. Plus, the more open design provided economic advantages by reducing construction costs and by allow-

ing the same space to be used for multiple programs during the week.

Whether a church is evaluating its existing building, meeting in a temporary facility (school, warehouse, etc.), or planning a new structure, building use must be decided in light of the purposes of the programs. Space for instructional purposes should be planned to support the church's ministry and educational philosophy. How people learn determines how we teach; and how we teach determines what kind of room we need.

At the same time, all educational space in a church should be planned to allow for multiple use, preferably among compatible age groups. Rooms for children and youth should accommodate Sunday school classes, youth groups, clubs, day school, after school care, and so on. Rooms for adults should accommodate all types of classes and study groups, fellowship activities, missions and service groups, committees, and so on.

Age Level Flexibility

In conducting a busy church's various programs, it is most efficient to have similar age groups use the same rooms as much as possible. Early childhood rooms tend to be the most difficult to adapt to accommodate other ages because of the size of furnishings and the specialized equipment needed. When building or remodeling, it is wise to plan space so most rooms could easily be changed to accommodate any age group.

Age Level Rooms

Rooms of at least 800-900 square feet are described as standard. This size room (and up to 1200 sq. ft.) works well because it accommodates the maximum group numbers that are desirable for any age level. The standard room size works for all age groups because the younger age groups need the smallest group sizes and the largest amount of floor space per person. Older age levels can accommodate larger groups, but do not need as much space per person.

The worksheet on pages 171 and 172 will provide additional information on room specifications.

Sharing Facilities

Providing flexibility without sacrificing effectiveness is a major challenge for ministries that share facilities and equipment. When two or more programs (e.g., Sunday school and day school) use the same space, sometimes the sharing process can be as tense as two preschoolers competing for the same toy. One program may be treated like an undesirable tenant or a minor appendage. The following guidelines help the leaders and staff of two or more programs to work in harmony even when they feel crowded in the available space.

1. Meet together to share the goals of each group. Problems are much easier to resolve when the people involved have established a relationship and agree that the building is not "owned" by any program. Facilities are shared resources that must be used to help each group fulfill its mission in the life of the church.

2. Mutually develop a plan that identifies any equipment and supplies that are to be shared and any items that are reserved for one group only.

3. Hang reversible bulletin boards; allow each group to use one side for its displays. Otherwise, designate some boards for each group. If renting space, portable display boards are useful so

teachers can mount visual material and then store it safely.

4. If a day school shares the facilities, provide student tables with removable tote trays instead of individual do desks. Tables allow more room arrangements and group activities than desks. Using the same furniture for the two programs avoids major custodial work every week.

5. Provide adequate storage space for each program. Cabinets with doors and locks are desirable. If a group's unique supplies must be removed from the room after the session, provide sturdy, portable containers that teachers can easily carry in and out.

Furniture and Equipment

Chairs and Tables

Chairs and tables are the bread and butter of classroom equipment. All age groups need chairs. Early childhood and children's rooms need tables. Youth and adult classes enjoy working around tables when space permits. Consider the following guidelines in selecting tables and chairs for various age groups. Also, see the chart on page 172.

1. Tables and chairs should be the right size for the age group. Learning suffers and relationship building is hindered when people are uncomfortably seated.

2. If the numbers of people in a room vary significantly for the various programs that use the room (i.e., thirty adults during Sunday school, twenty at an evening elective, and ten for a midweek support group), unused chairs should be easily stored out of sight, or at least out of the way. Group dynamics suffer when participants are surrounded by empty chairs.

3. Choose tables of a size that will

comfortably seat the number of people who can effectively interact with each other. For example, avoid using a table that can accommodate twelve two-year-olds, since there are no activities that twelve two-year-olds can do together. Two or three smaller tables would be more efficient and flexible. (Also, large tables are difficult to move, so they limit variety in room arrangements.)

4. The shape of the tabletops should fit the activities most likely to be done with them. Choose rectangular tables for children who use the tables for completing work sheets and art projects. Round tables are excellent for youth and adult classes where fellowship and discussion are the most frequent group activities. If a room is crowded, tables may need to be removed.

Additional Furniture and Equipment

A comfortable environment that is conducive to effective learning usually includes other important furniture and equipment. While it is possible to get by without any of these items, properly equipped rooms make the teacher's job easier and facilitate group interaction and individual learning. The list that follows identifies the most common items used at each age level.

Computers

While computers have become important parts of most public school classes, their use as a classroom resource in most churches is limited due to cost and lack of appropriate software. Where computers have become very important, however, is in helping leaders manage information on those who are attending. Computers are helping churches to quickly record people's attendance, to identify absentees and visitors needing to be contacted, and to print letters, memos, and reminders that aid in communication.

Room Arrangements

Furniture and equipment should be easy to rearrange for a balance of both small-group interaction and large group presentations. If moving between activities is too difficult, teachers may not expend the effort to provide a variety of learning experiences.

Open space is necessary in every classroom. People are hindered from informal dialogue and fellowship when a room is filled with furniture. When learners are involved in small group interaction, open space between groups acts as a buffer and helps learners focus on their particular group.

Room arrangement diagrams are on pages 173-176.

Curriculum and Other Resources

While classroom design, space, and furnishings are important, no one ever learned much about the Christian life from the walls, floor, or furniture. At the beginning of this chapter, the point was made that a church should shape its facilities by the church's programs, rather than allowing the facility to shape the programs. The key component in helping a church determine the "shape" of its educational ministries is the curriculum chosen to guide teachers and leaders in their ministry. Curriculum materials not only define what to teach, they also lay out the pattern for how to teach.

Trying to initiate or maintain a desired approach to educational ministries without having curriculum that supports and reinforces that approach may be only slightly more difficult than trying to build bricks without straw (Exodus 5) or threshing wheat in a winepress (Judges 6). Curriculum is essential to guide teachers, session after session, in implementing the objectives of the teaching ministry. Without such resources, teachers and leaders will muddle along, working in a variety of ways to fulfill a variety of goals, and they will accomplish little cooperation and momentum.

Choosing the best curriculum for a church is not simple. Each lesson for each age level contains numerous features and factors: Aims, content, methods, graphics, teacher helps, learner involvement aids, theological and denominational emphases, age-level appropriateness, and so on. These factors can be mind-boggling to someone who is trying to evaluate it and to compare it to other sources. Suffice it to say that some people who have gone through a curriculum selection process claim it is slightly more enjoyable than a root canal.

Since churches realize the tremendous influence that curriculum has on their educational ministries, periodically they ask someone to choose material. The following are perhaps the ten *worst* reasons for adopting a particular curriculum.

1. It's what we've always used; or it's different from what we've always used. (Consistency is a virtue, but if that's the best reason anyone can come up with for continuing to do something, things are pretty stagnant. Change is good, but change for the sake of change is not necessarily progress. Different is not always better.)

2. We're desperate for a teacher, and Mrs. Jones said she'd do it if she could pick her own materials. (If necessity is the mother of invention, desperation is often the father of disaster. Unless Mrs. Jones' favored materials meet your church's standards, you could be gaining a teacher and losing a program.)

3. They'll give us a free quarter of curriculum if we switch. (There's no such thing as a free lunch, or a free quarter. You may end up paying for it by being obligated to use materials you would not have chosen otherwise. If you wouldn't use it if you had to pay for it, don't use it.)

4. It's what they use at Church A. (Remember David in Saul's armor? What works for Church A may not fit the needs of Church B.)

5. This publisher's materials are very good for another age group. (Publishers don't produce peas in a pod. Just because one age level's material is good does not automatically mean the materials for another age level are as well done.)

6. I like their art the best. (A picture may be worth a thousand words, but beauty must be more than skin deep. Appealing pictures do not compensate if the philosophy, content, and methodology do not aid your staff in fulfilling your goals.)

7. Their ads say it's easy to use. (All curriculum ads claim ease of use. While it's a valid factor to consider, there's a point where things can get so easy—just glance over this page, and you're ready to go—that little or no impact will result. If your objective is to conduct classes expending the least amount of effort possible, that's one thing. If you yearn to see your ministries make a lasting difference in people's lives, that's another matter entirely.)

8. It's written just for our type of church. (It's probably not the only one that addresses your church's objectives. And of those, it may not do the best job

for you. Picking curriculum just because of its label may isolate you from other quality resources that could be more effective.)

9. They're all pretty much the same, so we just picked one. (If you're not particular about what you accomplish, then this approach is probably as good as any other.)

10. We've decided to write our own. (Why not reinvent the wheel while we're at it? Only a fraction of the amount of time, creativity, and energy necessary to produce even mediocre curriculum would be needed to adapt or enrich some of the fine quality resources already available.)

How then should a church compare curriculum options? How can a leader or committee determine which resources to use? One approach is to rate curriculum on various factors, weighing the importance of each factor in light of the church's goals. The curriculum evaluation worksheet on pages 177 and 178 can help with this task.

Resource Room and Storage Space

There are two kinds of people in the world: those who keep and those who throw. Keepers hang onto things in case they may need them someday. Throwers identify things they haven't used for a long time and get rid of them (usually just before they could have used them again).

These two types of people usually end up married to each other or working together in the Sunday school. Therefore, supply rooms, closets, cupboards, or file cabinets used to store supplies have the potential to create conflicts over what to keep and what to throw away.

This manual definitely sides with the throwers. Storage space in most churches is usually inadequate. Cluttering it with items "we might need someday" usually guarantees that no one will be able to find them when they are needed because they will be stacked underneath numerous other items also being saved for some future event. In the meantime, there's little or no space for efficiently storing the resources teachers need on an ongoing basis. These ongoing resources should be given priority in allotting storage space.

Easy access and efficient organization are essential for resources and supplies. If teachers have to arrive early and then conduct an intensive search for materials, they are likely to avoid learning procedures that use any but the most basic materials. This results in a lack of variety followed by reduced learner involvement followed by lower interest and diminished learning.

The Resources and Storage worksheet on pages 179 and 180 is helpful for evaluating resources and storage.

A Facility Overview

Mark the actions to rate your present and planned efforts for your facilities.

E=Excellent
S=Satisfactorily Doing Now
I=Improvement Needed
N=Need to Start

Fit Facilities to Philosophy

_____ 1. Facilities are planned for workable group sizes in which all learners can comfortably build relationships and engage in active learning.

_____ 2. Room sizes and arrangements are planned to facilitate observation and to help leaders support the staff.

_____ 3. Buildings are designed to provide easy access by everyone, with special attention given to the needs of first-time visitors, parents with small children, the elderly, and people with physical handicaps.

Make Facilities Personal

_____ 1. All areas of buildings are regularly evaluated to ensure that the physical and social needs of learners are accommodated.

_____ 2. Floor coverings (carpet, tile, linoleum, wood) are easy to clean and, in children's rooms, are appropriate for sitting on the floor. (Carpet has the advantage of absorbing sound and retaining warmth. As much as possible, use the same type of floor covering throughout a building. When both carpet and tile are in a building, one or the other may not get cleaned regularly due to the extra work.)

_____ 3. Walls are painted in inviting, restful colors with accented areas such as bulletin boards, chalkboards, and so on. Displays are mounted at eye level for the age group using the room and are kept up to date to reflect current areas of study and interest. (While there is value in allowing youth rooms to reflect the typically off-beat proclivities of young people, it is also important to furnish and maintain these rooms so they convey a sense of value.)

_____ 4. Ceilings lights give adequate, even illumination balanced with outside light when available. (It is helpful if lights can be dimmed and windows covered when watching a video, using an overhead projector, during rest time, etc.)

_____ 5. Electrical outlets are placed for convenient use with several outlets on each wall. (In early childhood rooms outlets should be placed at table

or counter height so they, as well as plugs and cords, are out of the reach of children. Plug guards should cover any unused plugs.)

Mark the actions to rate your present and planned efforts for your facilities.

E=Excellent
S=Satisfactorily
    Doing Now
I=Improvement Needed
N=Need to Start

_____ 6. Separate heating and ventilation controls are provided for rooms in each zone.

_____ 7. Early childhood rooms have direct access to child-size rest rooms. The number of sinks and toilets follow state or local guidelines for the number of children to be served. Rest rooms for older children, youth, and adults are located near their classrooms and have adequate facilities to handle between-service congestion.

_____ 8. An evacuation plan is in place for all classrooms and hallways in case of fire, earthquake, or other disaster.

_____ 9. Hallway congestion before and after a session has been considered in planning the location of groups. For example, early childhood rooms are located where parents can easily deliver and pick up children.

_____ 10. All areas of the buildings offer easy access for people with handicaps.

Room Specifications

Mark the actions to rate your present and planned efforts to make your facilities accommodate the needs of all age levels.

E=Excellent
S=Satisfactorily
Doing Now
I=Improvement Needed
N=Need to Start

Flexibility

_____ 1. We have standard size rooms (800-900 sq. ft.) that work well for any age level. When groups are smaller, these rooms are easily divided in halves or thirds by installing nonbearing walls that are taken out when bigger rooms are needed.

_____ 2. We use movable walls between rooms when necessary to create larger open space. (The up-front investment in quality dividers is worth the savings gained by making your facility flexible for current needs as well as for future changes you may not be able to anticipate.)

_____ 3. We provide ample storage for each program. (A church that wants to get multiple use out of its facilities must provide plenty of convenient storage for the various age groups and programs that use any room. Closed cabinets that are mounted about shoulder height and up work best for storing supplies between sessions. Low open shelves are very helpful for placing materials to be used during the session.)

Room Sizes

* The maximum attendance numbers assume adequate teacher-to-learner ratios are maintained.

Age Group	Space Per Person	Maximum Attendance*	Room Size	Teacher: Learner Ratio
Early Childhood				
Ages 0-12 mo.	35 sq. ft.	15	600-900 sq. ft.	1:2
Ages 12-24 mo.	35 sq. ft.	15	600-900 sq. ft.	1:2
Ages 2-3 years	35 sq. ft.	16	700-900 sq. ft.	1:3
Ages 4-6 years	35 sq. ft.	20	800-900 sq. ft.	1:4
Children				
Grades 1-2	30 sq. ft.	25	800-900 sq. ft.	1:6
Grades 3-6	30 sq. ft.	30	900 sq. ft.	1:8
Youth				
Grades 6-12	25 sq. ft.	40	900-1000 sq. ft.	1:8
Adult				
Ages 18+	15 sq. ft.	40	600-900 sq. ft.	1:8

- Early Childhood: One teacher per two to four children, depending on ages
- Children: One teacher per six to eight children
- Youth: One teacher per eight students
- Adult: One teacher or leader per eight adults

(*Chapter 4 contains details on teacher-to-learner ratios and group sizes.*)

If a room is smaller than 800 square feet, reduce the maximum attendance numbers proportionately. Smaller rooms reduce the options for certain learning activities, especially if the recommended square footage per person cannot be provided. For example, in early childhood rooms, two valuable learning centers that require significant amounts of floor space are family living (where children role-play typical family life experiences) and block building (where children learn to work together cooperatively). When adequate floor space is not available, these activities become difficult, if not impossible, to provide.

Slightly rectangular classrooms tend to be most efficient and flexible. Proportions approximating three-by-four (i.e., twenty-five feet wide by thirty-six feet long) work very well for a variety of room arrangements.

Chair and Table Sizes

Age Group	Chair Height (seat above floor)	Table Height	Table Top
Early Childhood	10-12 inches	20-22 inches	30" x 48"
Children	14-16 inches	22-26 inches	36" x 60"
Youth and Adult	18 inches	(optional) 28 inches	Round: 72" diameter Rectangular: 36" x 96"

Room Arrangement Diagrams

Babies' Room

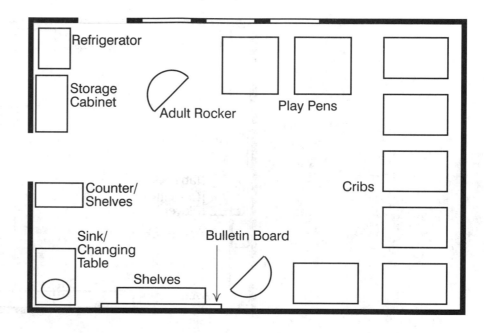

Toddlers' Room

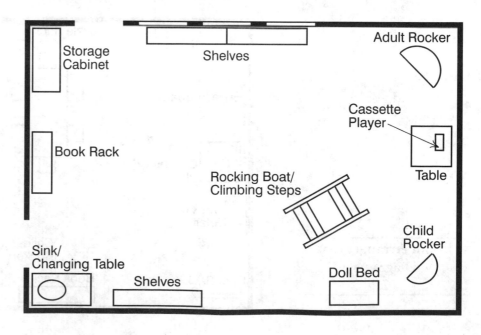

Room Arrangement Diagrams

2's and 3's Room

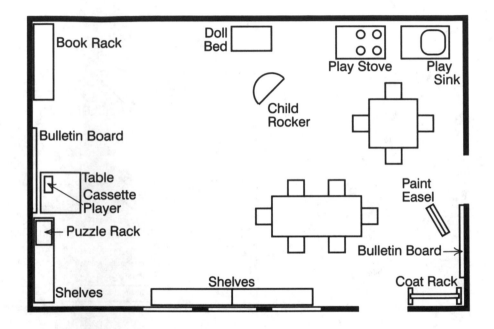

4's and 5's Room

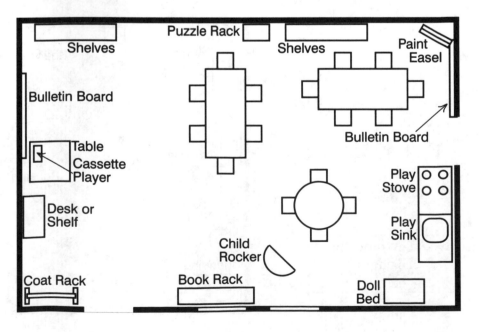

Room Arrangement Diagrams

Children's Classroom/Assembly Arrangement

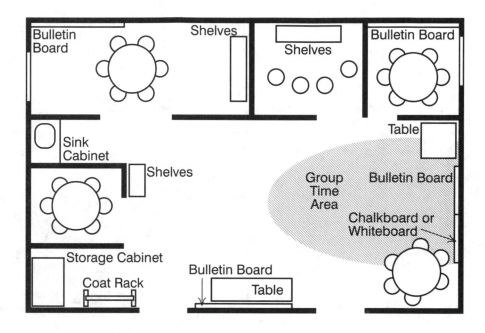

Children's Open Room Arrangement

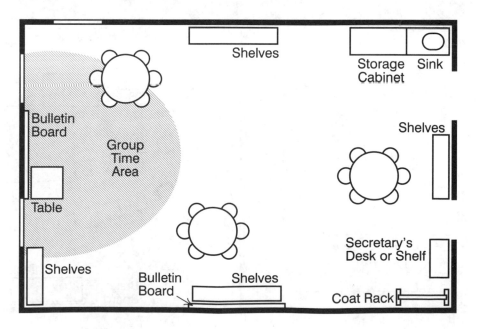

Room Arrangement Diagrams

Youth/Adult Room With Tables

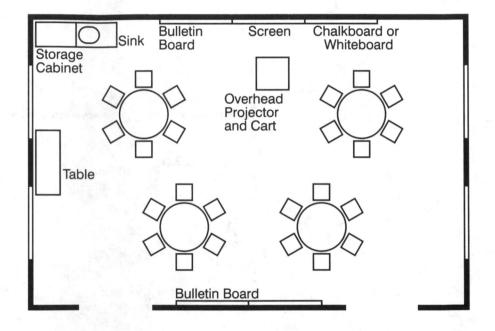

Youth/Adult Classroom - No Tables

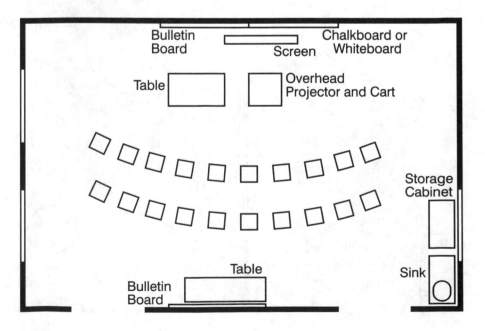

Curriculum Evaluation Worksheet

Publisher: _____

Course Evaluated: _____ Age Level: _____

Evaluator: _____

Rating Scale

Strong   Weak

1 2 3 4 5 6 7

1 2 3 4 5 6 7

1 2 3 4 5 6 7

1 2 3 4 5 6 7
1 2 3 4 5 6 7

1 2 3 4 5 6 7

1 2 3 4 5 6 7

1 2 3 4 5 6 7

1 2 3 4 5 6 7

1 2 3 4 5 6 7

1 2 3 4 5 6 7

1 2 3 4 5 6 7

1 2 3 4 5 6 7

1. Objectives

a. Lessons and units have clearly defined objectives, stating in measurable terms (not vague generalities) what learners will do as evidence of their learning.

b. Learning activities are suggested in each lesson that lead to the accomplishment of the stated objectives.

c. Objectives are supportive of the goals established for the church's educational ministries.

2. Theological Emphasis

a. The major doctrines our church wants to teach are clearly presented.

b. Lesson content reflects an appreciation of essential truths as taught by our church.

c. Examples and illustrations include church situations that are familiar to our people.

3. Biblical Interpretation

a. The Bible is clearly presented as God's authoritative and reliable Word to all people.

b. Lessons accurately present the teachings of Scripture passages being studied and do not impose arbitrary or external interpretations.

c. Learners are encouraged and given frequent opportunities to explore the Scriptures themselves.

4. Life Application

a. All lessons guide learners to consider for their own lives the practical implications of the truths being studied.

b. Ample time is provided in the session plan for both examination of content and consideration of applying the content to life.

c. All lessons provide learning activities that effectively move learners toward putting the lesson truths into practice.

5. Methodology

a. All lessons provide a balance of learning procedures, including both input from the teacher and active learner involvement.

Strong   Weak

1 2 3 4 5 6 7   b. Throughout the duration of a course, a variety of learning activities is provided to accommodate the varied learning styles of participants.

1 2 3 4 5 6 7   c. The suggested methods are ones that most teachers and learners find comfortable and are a mixture of ideas designed to encourage healthy creativity and innovation.

6. Flexibility

1 2 3 4 5 6 7   a. Session plans provide ample alternatives to fit a variety of class situations and teaching skills.

1 2 3 4 5 6 7   b. Suggestions and tips are provided to aid teachers in effectively using or adapting the ideas presented.

1 2 3 4 5 6 7   c. Ideas are given so teachers can offer appropriate choices to learners in order to meet the distinct needs of individuals.

7. Age-Level Appropriateness

1 2 3 4 5 6 7   a. Content to be taught is appropriate to the experiences and interests of the selected age level.

1 2 3 4 5 6 7   b. Adequate help is given the teacher for ways to help students understand lesson content.

1 2 3 4 5 6 7   c. Learning activities fit the abilities and attitudes of the age level.

8. Preparation Procedures

1 2 3 4 5 6 7   a. Each lesson provides guidance for the teacher's own personal and spiritual growth in response to the content to be taught.

1 2 3 4 5 6 7   b. Materials and supplies suggested for use in the sessions are inexpensive and readily obtained and prepared.

1 2 3 4 5 6 7   c. Preparation of each lesson can easily be done within a reasonable time, enabling the average teacher to feel confident in approaching the session.

9. Appearance and Visual Appeal

1 2 3 4 5 6 7   a. All materials intended for use by learners are visually attractive and designed appropriately for the intended age level.

1 2 3 4 5 6 7   b. All materials intended for use by teachers are presented in a consistent, easy-to-read format.

1 2 3 4 5 6 7   c. Graphics, photographs, and art accurately illustrate biblical settings and consistently reflect the full diversity of contemporary people to whom the church is called to minister.

10. Cost and Value

1 2 3 4 5 6 7   a. The price of the materials fairly represents the quality and workmanship of the products.

1 2 3 4 5 6 7   b. The benefits the curriculum provides balance the cost.

1 2 3 4 5 6 7   c. The cost of the materials fits within the amount we truly believe we should be investing in this ministry.

Resources and Storage

Mark the actions to rate your present and planned efforts to provide adequate resources to teachers and leaders.

E=Excellent
S=Satisfactorily
    Doing Now
I=Improvement Needed
N=Need to Start

In-Class Storage

_____ 1. Adequate (enclosed and secured) space is provided for all groups. Supplies used on a regular basis are stored in the group's room.

Early Childhood and Children

__ scissors (child-sized, two or three adult-sized)
__ glue (white glue, glue sticks)
__ crayons
__ washable markers (fine, wide tipped)
__ erasable markers for white board (if one is used)
__ transparent tape
__ masking tape
__ pencils

__ chalk (white, colored)
__ writing paper
__ construction paper, various colors (9" x 12")
__ white shelf paper (12" to 18" roll)
__ index cards (3" x 5" and 4" x 6")
__ name tags
__ stapler and staples
— _____
— _____

Youth and Adult

__ markers (fine, wide tipped)
__ erasable markers for white board (if one is used)
__ overhead transparency pens (if overhead is used)
__ blank transparencies (if needed)
__ clear adhesive tape
__ masking tape
__ pencils

__ chalk (white, colored)
__ writing paper
__ white shelf paper (12" to 18" roll)
__ index cards (3" x 5" and 4" x 6")
__ name tags
__ stapler and staples
— _____
— _____

_____ 2. If two or more groups using the same room use similar supplies, a clearly defined plan is in place for sharing those resources or keeping them separate.

_____ 3. If in-class storage is not available for supplies used regularly, an appropriate container (i.e., sturdy cardboard portable file box) is provided along with an easily accessible place for storing the container between sessions.

Supply Room and Workroom

_____ 1. Audio visual equipment that is not kept in classrooms is stored and cataloged for easy access and check-out procedures. Typical items provided include:

__ audio cassette players
__ overhead projector
__ overhead cart
__ video cassette player/monitor
__ video camera

__ video cart
__ video projection unit (for large rooms)
— _____

Mark the actions to rate your present and planned efforts to provide adequate resources to teachers and leaders.

E=Excellent
S=Satisfactorily
Doing Now
I=Improvement Needed
N=Need to Start

_____ 2. Resource books and tapes are provided here or in the church library depending on which is most accessible to teachers. Types of resources provided include:

___ Bible dictionaries and encyclopedias for each age level
___ Bible atlases for each age level
___ Dictionaries for each age level
___ Song books
___ Music tapes
___ Teacher training videos
___ Idea books (learning activities, crafts, skits, etc.)
___ Bible story videos
___ _____
___ _____

_____ 3. An easily accessible location is available to teachers where they can restock their regular supplies.

_____ 4. This location also provides supplies that are too large to store easily in the classroom and that are used less frequently. This includes items

___ construction paper, various colors (12" x 18")
___ poster board, various colors (12" x 18" and 18" x 24")
___ newsprint (on roll or sheets of 18" x 24" and 24" x 36")
___ butcher and art paper (on roll, both white and colored)
___ clear adhesive plastic or laminating equipment and supplies
___ paper cutter
___ assorted fabric pieces
___ assorted fabric trim (e.g., rick rack)
___ yarn, string, rope
___ paint supplies (tempera paints, brushes, smocks)
___ thumbtacks
___ paper clips
___ paper fasteners
___ paper punch
___ chenille wire
___ paper bags (lunch, grocery size)
___ first aid kit
___ blank audio cassettes
___ rhythm instruments
___ autoharp
___ clean up items (sponges, disposable wipes, paper towels, vacuum, carpet sweeper, etc.)
___ Bible-times costumes
___ Picture file
___ _____
___ _____

_____ 5. Adequate space is provided (and kept free of storage and clutter) so that teachers can spread out materials and work.

_____ 6. A responsible person is in charge of keeping these supplies and resources well stocked and in good working order as well as ensuring that teachers have access to them when needed. (A common problem with people placed in charge of a resource room is the tendency to value neatness and order over open access and use. While order is essential, it must be seen as an aid to usefulness, not as an end in itself. The resource room should never become a museum to be admired.)

_____ 7. Supplies and resources are a regular part of the church's budget. Provisions are made for purchases and maintenance.

9 *Building Small Groups*

Perhaps the best place to begin a consideration of small group ministries is with some definition of terms. First, the term small can be applied to groups of people in several ways:

√ short of stature (definitely not referring to the Boston Celtics);

√ mean, petty, ungenerous (obviously not the co-workers of Mother Theresa);

√ few in number (certainly not the congregation at the Crystal Cathedral or Willow Creek).

In this chapter, the term *small* is used with the latter meaning. But that raises the question, how small is *small*? Compared to the congregations at many megachurches, almost any group of people could be considered small. The use of the term *small* in this chapter is limited to groups that are small enough to meet the following criteria:

- Everyone in the group can easily get to know everyone else.
- A person will be missed by the group (not just the host or secretary) if he/she is not there.
- Everyone can feel comfortable in talking aloud during the group sessions.
- Everyone can develop a sense of responsibility to everyone else in the group.

How small is that? In most groups that meet once a week, the term *small* cannot be stretched beyond about twelve to fifteen people.

Now that small has been clarified, let's tackle *group*. A *group* is not just a collection of people who happen to be together in the same place at the same time. Nine people in an elevator, fourteen people on an airport tram, twelve people gathered around a coffee urn in the church fellowship hall are not really groups.

A group needs the following elements:

- A sense of identity as a group (matching T-shirts are not necessary);
- Regular opportunities for deepening relationships;
- A shared purpose for being together.

Two down, let's go for three: *Ministries.* Christians tend to label many things as ministries without giving much thought to the term. Just as *fellowship* means much more than getting together for a good time, and *Bible study* is more than a class passively listening to a teacher give a report on his study during the week, *ministry* is not a catchall term for anything a group of Christians might do.

Ministry includes the following:

- Service (actions growing out of a sense of love and duty for others);
- Stewardship for Christ (consciously using time and effort as offerings to him);
- Discipleship (seeking to grow in understanding of what God's purposes are and how to become more fully involved in those purposes).

Perhaps, after reading these definitions, you think that this chapter will not apply to your program.

- Your groups may not be small.
- Your people may not be a group.
- Your programs may not be seen as ministry.

Before you skip the rest of this chapter, consider these significant ways that this chapter can help you.

- Your large groups may significantly increase their effectiveness by forming into small groups at times.
- Your people (even your rugged individualists) may discover personal benefits in becoming part of a meaningful group.
- Your programs may be greatly enhanced by building an awareness of the potential for ministry.

Values of Small Groups

Why are small group ministries important in the life of every church? Here are some reasons.

- They give people a sense of belonging that counters the loneliness created by an impersonal society.
- They provide encouragement and caring from people who have become significant to one another.
- They demand accountability because group members help one another apply Christian principles in daily living.
- They aid involvement, which is the most effective means the church can use to help people over their reluctance to participate.

Purposes of Small Groups

Most small groups exist primarily as a means of outreach to non-Christians or as a source of growth for Christians. While many groups may seek to accomplish both outreach and nurture, one or the other usually dominates. Whichever dominant purpose a group has, there is also usually a specific approach by which the group seeks to achieve that purpose.

• Some groups focus on fellowship, perhaps meeting to get better acquainted through a common interest (sports, music, fishing, cooking, etc.).

• Some groups major in studying together. They may study the Bible, a doctrine, a particular book, an issue, or a topic.

• Other groups emphasize providing spiritual and practical support for one another. These groups may consist of people with a common need (divorce recovery, single parents, domestic abuse, etc.) and usually include significant time for group prayer and sharing.

• Every church has groups that exist to fulfill specific tasks. These are usually called boards or committees and also include choirs, visitation teams, Sunday school teachers, mission support groups, and so on.

No matter what purpose or area of concern a small group has, all four of the above functions need to be included in the group's life in order for it to be effective in ministry.

Type of Group	Nurture	Outreach
Sharing and Fellowship	X	X
Study	X	X
Support and Prayer	X	X
Service and Task	X	X

Sharing and fellowship are necessary components of any small group ministry.

• Through sharing and fellowship, people get to know one another and develop a sense of belonging.

• Trust is built that will enable the group to study, pray, and serve together.

These results of sharing and fellowship do not occur just by plugging in the coffee pot and giving everyone a donut or carrot stick. While it is valuable to have people mingle and chat and chew, the time comes when some planned interaction must occur in order to help the group

become aware that everyone shares some common bonds. A group's leaders must take the initiative to encourage healthy sharing about things that really matter, not just the latest sports scores, stock quotes, or fashion trends.

Study is essential for every small group.

• It builds up the individuals within the group.

• It helps a group focus on its real purpose within the church.

• Even a brief time of appropriate Bible study builds understanding of the group's ministry.

It is easy to see the value of study for a group that exists for that purpose. Even a group that meets to pull weeds in the church parking lot can benefit from a few minutes consideration of a passage about the value of work or service. Many groups that meet for a purpose other than study are so anxious to get on to the task at hand that reading and talking about the Bible can seem like a needless diversion. However, there is no shortcut to building a solid awareness of biblical guidelines for the things we do as God's people. Group study of a carefully chosen passage can greatly enhance the effectiveness of any group's efforts.

Careful thought must be given to making group study effective. This is essential because most people have encountered the Bible in either a large group setting or as an individual in private devotions. Leading study in a small group calls for some unique approaches that take full advantage of the setting, engaging people in cooperative, supportive learning.

Support and prayer involve much more than opening or closing a session with a word of prayer. Effective small groups develop a sense of community in which praying for one another is the springboard for real caring. Groups succeed in this area when the leaders understand and communicate the following:

- People need a safe environment in which to express and respond to needs.
- People of all types of backgrounds can be led into meaningful times of prayer in a small group.
- Prayer is not just asking God to do what we want, but allowing God to work in us to help us do what he wants.
- Deep meaningful caring within the group is an essential foundation in equipping the group members to minister outside the group.

Service is rarely thought of as a group function in most groups that emphasize fellowship, study, or support. However, any group that does not consciously reach out beyond its own members will quickly stagnate and become ingrown.

- Fellowship groups need to be led into service to keep from becoming mere social groups with a religious flavor.
- Study groups need to apply what they have learned to some practical expression. This keeps each group member's faith from being only an academic exercise.
- Support and prayer groups need to move into some type of service to keep from becoming self-centered cliques or spiritual recluses.

Involving a group in a service or outreach project is one of the most effective ways to help people discover that their faith is effective. Far too many Christians have been challenged to live for Christ, but they have been sent out on their own and have been defeated. Most people need the support and encouragement of a team effort in order to see their faith have an impact beyond the comfortable confines of the church. The goal is to lead a group into an area of ministry beyond themselves.

Environments for Small Groups

Where a group meets has a significant impact on the dynamics that operate within the group. Expectations, attitudes, behaviors, and results are all influenced by surroundings. Observe a group of teenagers hanging out on a street corner, seated in their favorite fast food restaurant, and grouped around a table in the library. In most cases, the noise level, the physical movement, the group interaction, and the topics of conversation are noticeably different at each location.

Groups That Meet at the Church Building

Church buildings provide many advantages as meeting places for small groups.

- They are familiar, often central, locations for church members.
- They have available resources to aid the group's purposes (equipment, supplies, furniture, etc.).
- The rooms are large enough to accommodate large groups (i.e., Sunday school departments and classes) that can form into small groups for parts of their time together.
- The proximity to other church and family functions can be convenient as well as a reminder of the group's relationship to the larger body.

Groups that meet at the church building often need to deal with some potential problems involving their meeting place.

- Rooms may not be designed to encourage small group interaction and cohesion. (Metal folding chairs and long banquet tables do little to encourage comfort or intimacy.) Often rooms at the church building must serve a variety of purposes and no one takes the initiative to prepare the room adequately.

- People who are not part of the church often feel uncomfortable meeting there.
- People who are part of the church may associate the locations with the large-group experiences they have had there and find it difficult to participate in small group processes.
- Leaders may assume this is just another church meeting and proceed with business as usual, not giving attention to the unique needs of small groups.
- People may attend a group out of convenience, not from a desire to pursue the group's goals. This is especially true if the group meets at the same time that a family member's program meets.

These problems can be minimized by doing the following:

- Make the room as comfortable and attractive as possible.
- Designate someone in the group to prepare the room before the session. (This task could be rotated among group members or assumed by someone willing to be host.)
- Emphasize sharing activities to build community within the group.
- Accept people regardless of their reason for coming, then make the group as meaningful as possible in order to reach each person at a deeper level.

Groups That Meet in Homes

Christians have been meeting together in homes since the book of Acts. Homes provide significant benefits as settings for small groups.

- Friendliness and warmth tend to be two main characteristics people appreciate about meeting in a home.
- Cost-effectiveness is a quality church building committees like, since home groups do not require construction or maintenance of added church facilities.
- Since the home is where people live, home groups often aid in putting faith into action in daily living.

Homes also have a few potential drawbacks as meeting places.

- They may be difficult to locate the first time and parking can be a problem in some neighborhoods. (This is not a problem for a neighborhood group where everyone lives nearby.)
- Many homes do not have comfortable seating for a dozen or so people in one room. Sometimes the host must secure additional chairs. (Apartments and condominiums that have an activity room can often accommodate groups very comfortably.)
- Child care needs can pose problems for parents who are used to the convenience of a church nursery and other children's programs at the church building.
- Some people are reluctant to open their homes to a group since they feel pressure to clean house before company comes and to prepare and serve elaborate refreshments.

These problems can be minimized by doing the following:

- Provide maps or printed directions with suggestions where to park.

- Fit the size of group to the capacity of the home, not trying to fit a group of fifteen into a living room for eight.
- Offer child care at the church building or a nearby home, or compile a list of nearby baby-sitters whom parents can contact.
- Discourage house tours by group members so hosts only have to straighten the rooms the group will use.
- Set a clear policy on the type of refreshments to be served and rotate responsibility for preparation among the group members.

Groups That Meet at an Office, Workshop, or Restaurant

Many small groups meet in the community, using facilities where people work or meet. These locations are usually chosen because they are convenient, familiar, and comfortable to the participants. These groups sometimes are limited by lack of privacy and by the size of the meeting place. (How many people can squeeze into an office or a restaurant booth?) However, their location is often a strong plus in leading people to follow through on things discussed in the group.

Levels of Small Groups

Every church has people who are at widely different levels of spiritual growth and whose needs from a small group also differ greatly. Therefore, a church needs to think about a spectrum of small-group levels that can meet this range of needs. One way of approaching this is to rate all the existing events and groups within the church by the level of initial threat and commitment involved in getting into the group. Consider putting a numerical value

on each event or group, estimating the level of threat and commitment across a spectrum like the one on page 189.

The threat level for an unchurched person of any group will vary significantly depending on how well he/she knows the leader and other people in the group.

The commitment level will also vary depending on the duration of the group, the amount of preparation required, and the expectations for consistency in participation.

This chart is provided to encourage your church to evaluate whether or not its groups offer enough variety in their threat and commitment levels. (It is not a list of the kinds of groups a church should have.) People who have progressed to involvement at deeper levels can be intolerant of groups that function at less-intense levels. Someone who desires in-depth discipleship may disparage a Sunday school class because he/she perceives little carry-over from week to week. It is often necessary to explain to these people the need for the church to minister to all people, accepting them where they are and then leading them to grow from that point.

Starting Small Groups

Every small group develops its own personality that reflects the characteristics of the various members of the group. Because of this, a church's strategy for developing small group ministries needs to reflect the unique qualities within that congregation and not merely try to emulate what another church has done successfully.

A wise church will follow more than one strategy in order to make small groups fit the needs and personality of the congregation and the community. Consider these approaches.

Create Groups Within Groups

Examine your existing groups to see which ones may benefit by forming into smaller groups at certain times. For example, an adult Sunday school class of thirty members could easily form three or four care groups that could work together during class as directed by the teacher and with guidance from a group leader. Adult care groups could also meet separately during each week (or month) to build stronger group relationships.

Small groups within large groups are strengthened by the connection to the large group.

- Group leaders can receive support from the class teacher.
- Group members maintain relationships with more than just the members of their small group.
- The large group serves as an important bridge between the small group and the rest of the congregation. By the same token, the large group benefits when it forms smaller units.
- Group members learn better through the wider variety of learning procedures available when small group processes can be used as part of class sessions.
- Attendance increases as people develop a stronger sense of accountability through participation.
- The ministry of the teacher is expanded through the efforts of the small group leaders.

Enlist People to Join New Groups

Often churches need to begin totally new groups, and this usually requires enlisting people who are not currently involved in a group. This process includes these important steps.

- Compile a list of potential people for the new group(s).
- Enlist a group leader and host for each group. (See below.)
- Alert the congregation (or that segment of the congregation for whom the new group is intended) that a group will be formed soon. Explain the purposes, duration, and procedures of the group. Use bulletin, newsletter, and verbal announcements. Provide a registration form that people can fill out and return.
- Share with the congregation the experiences of people who have benefited from participation in a small group. Focus on one specific benefit in each testimonial.
- One or two weeks after these general announcements have been made, extend a personal invitation to each potential member. The group leader or host should make these contacts. Those who returned a registration form should also be contacted to confirm their participation in the group.

Connect People With Similar Needs and Interests

Often the most effective small groups are those initiated by people. This can occur when someone expresses a need or a desire to learn or serve in a particular area. The church leader who is made aware of this can do one of the following things:

- Put this person in touch with others who have already indicated they have the same need or interest.
- Work with this person to locate others with similar concerns.

Select and Enlist a Leader for the Group

No step in this process is more crucial than the selection and recruitment of the people who will lead the small groups. Several factors need to be kept in mind as this is done.

Make the selection and enlistment process a matter of prayer, asking God to identify and begin speaking to the people he wants to fulfill this task.

Prospective leaders need to be approached with the same personal concern that is desired for the leader to show towards members of the group. Mass appeals for help may be appropriate for some tasks, but not for enlisting people who are to personally guide the spiritual growth of others.

Small group leaders need to be people who have given evidence of their own desire to grow as Christians, but they do not need to be people who have arrived. They need to be people who have shown a desire to learn from the Scriptures, but they do not have to be authorities in biblical literature. The small group leader is to be a guide—even a fellow learner—not an expert with all the answers.

Choose and Adapt Appropriate Resources for Groups

Many adult group leaders, especially in groups that have study as their major focus, tend to pride themselves in not relying on any "canned curriculum." Their watchword is: "We just study the Bible." While this sounds commendable, some significant reasons exist why a church should provide Bible study resources to its small groups.

Inexperienced group leaders are intimidated by having to build their own session plans from scratch. However, they will quickly learn to lead if they observe other leaders working from the same resources they will be given. (Often church staff members provide poor models for new leaders by not using the available resources themselves. They explain that "I've been to seminary and I don't need that crutch," but in so doing, they leave their lay leaders with an unreachable example.)

Few leaders are skilled at both preparing the content for a study and developing effective group involvement procedures. The result far too often is a dull presentation. Good curriculum provides a leader with both sound biblical insights and proven methodology.

Most people who become Bible study leaders are serious students of the Word. While this is very helpful, it can also have a serious drawback in that the leader may assume everyone else in the group is at his/her level of Bible knowledge and interest. Thus, the sessions may focus heavily on content, and relationships may not be built. A good curriculum will provide a balanced approach to sharing and study.

In looking for effective small group resources, put these features high on your list of criteria.

- Accurate, focused treatment of Scripture that leads to specific life application;
- Appropriate and varied ideas for involving group members in studying the Bible on their own;
- Interesting suggestions for sharing and fellowship that will build relationships in the group.

(The "Curriculum Evaluation Worksheet" in Chapter 8 is a valid tool to help small group leaders compare features of several curricula.)

Levels of Small Groups

0 — **Low Threat and Commitment**
Adult social events
Invitation by church member to community activity
Allow children to attend church events

2 — **Minimal Threat and Commitment**
Worship service
Potluck dinner
Newcomers reception (an informal gathering hosted by minister)

4 — **Moderate Threat and Commitment**
Adult Sunday school classes
Newcomers get-acquainted series
Greeters or hospitality corps

6 — **Medium Threat and Commitment**
Church membership class
Home Bible study groups
Choir
Personal support groups

8 — **Significant Threat and Commitment**
Christian doctrines/Bible survey courses
Discipleship group
Church committees
Missions prayer groups

10 — **High Threat and Commitment**
Teaching Sunday school
Visitation teams
Church board

Is This Any Way to Run a Sunday School for the Next Hundred Years?

The ideas and guidelines presented in this manual may be antiquated and out-of-date by the end of the twenty-first century. (Assuming, of course, that the Lord delays the conclusion of human history until then.) These plans and procedures are not guaranteed to be timeless and remain valid through whatever unforeseen changes may come in the future.

In fact, the guidelines in this book are not even guaranteed to be the best way to run a Sunday school or other educational ministry today. Neither has this manual presented all the possible ways that people have found to teach and lead. However, the instructions in this manual are ways that really do work to organize and operate a Sunday school. And they work in churches of all sizes and types.

If you choose, having ploughed through this book, you can invest further time in exploring other approaches. There is certainly no shortage of capable, dedicated people who have applied themselves to writing such ideas. Although, "Of making many books there is no end, and much study wearies the body" (Ecclesiastes 12:12).

Or, you can roll up your sleeves and get to work, making your church a place where God's Word is taught with vision and imagination, motivating and guiding people of all ages to apply its truths to their lives.

This manual has provided a plan for your work.

Now it's time to work your plan.

191